Beginning WF

Windows Workflow in .NET 4.0

Mark J. Collins

Apress®

President and Publisher: Paul Manning
Lead Editor: Jonathan Hassell
Technical Reviewer: Michael Mayberry
Editorial Board: Clay Andres, Steve Anglin, Mark Beckner, Ewan Buckingham, Gary Cornell, Jonathan Gennick, Jonathan Hassell, Michelle Lowman, Matthew Moodie, Duncan Parkes, Jeffrey Pepper, Frank Pohlmann, Douglas Pundick, Ben Renow-Clarke, Dominic Shakeshaft, Matt Wade, Tom Welsh
Project Manager: Debra Kelly
Copy Editor: Nancy Sixsmith
Compositor: Laureltech
Indexer: BIM Indexing & Proofreading Services
Artist: April Milne
Cover Designer: Anna Ishchenko

Distributed to the book trade worldwide by Springer-Verlag New York, Inc., 233 Spring Street, 6th Floor, New York, NY 10013. Phone 1-800-SPRINGER, fax 201-348-4505, e-mail orders-ny@springer-sbm.com, or visit www.springeronline.com.

For information on translations, please e-mail rights@apress.com, or visit www.apress.com.

Apress and friends of ED books may be purchased in bulk for academic, corporate, or promotional use. eBook versions and licenses are also available for most titles. For more information, reference our Special Bulk Sales–eBook Licensing web page at www.apress.com/info/bulksales.

The source code for this book is available to readers at www.apress.com.

Dedicated to my wife, Donna. Your worth is far above rubies (Prov 31:10). I love you!

Contents at a Glance

Contents

About the Author

 **Mark Collins** wrote his first software program using Basic on the TRS-80 in 1978. As technology has evolved, so has his interest and enjoyment of this wonderful world of software. Mark's career has included many varied opportunities, including being an electrical engineer for IBM, being a system acquisition officer for the U.S. Air Force, spending 12 years designing and building world-class point-of-sale solutions, spending a two-year stint in Engand, and (most recently) providing donor management systems for two well-known nonprofit organizations. Mark has also developed a CASE tool called Omega Tool (www.TheCreativePeople.com).

About the Technical Reviewer

■ **Michael Mayberry** currently helps lead a software team for a nonprofit organization to build .NET enterprise applications. He serves as a lead architect and focuses on adopting new technologies toward solid solutions. Michael's experience includes the development of web-based extranet solutions, along with data collection and analysis applications within the auto industry. Michael moved to build CRM and BI solutions for the nonprofit industry more than seven years ago.

Acknowledgments

First of all, I want to acknowledge that anything that I have ever done that is of any value or significance was accomplished through the blessings of my Lord and Savior, Jesus Christ. This book is a visible demonstration of that fact. The challenges in a project such as this were beyond my own ability, and God's amazing grace carried me through. He is my strength, my vision, and my provider.

Next, I want to say a big "thank you" to my beautiful wife, Donna. You are an inspiration to me. You selflessly took care of our household and encouraged me to focus on this book. I could not have done it without you. You are the embodiment of a Proverbs 31 wife. I am truly blessed to be able to share my life with you.

I am also very thankful for all the people at Apress who made this book possible and for all their hard work that turned it into the finished product you see now. Through numerous rewrites and revisions you were always helpful, patient, and encouraging. Thank you!

I also want to thank Kevin Belknap, who helped me with the web application for the sample solution in the appendix. You always know how to make a site look great! Thank you for eagerly helping with this project.

Finally, I want to thank Michael Mayberry for reviewing this book. Not only did you review this book, but you also had to review several preliminary versions, which no one will probably ever see. I appreciate your heart that strives for excellence, your humility, and your selflessness.

Introduction

When I first started looking at Microsoft's Workflow Foundation (WF) I had a sense that there was something really useful there, but figuring out the right application of the technology seemed elusive. The available code samples demonstrated some specific features, but there was no roadmap to help bring it all together. So I started writing this book to help others who wanted to understand WF.

Along the way, the first beta release of WF 4.0 was made available, which was a complete departure from the previous version. So the first book based on version 3.5 was shelved, and I started writing a new book for WF 4.0. When the second Beta was released with significant changes, the book was once again rewritten. Having watched WF evolve from version 3.5 to 4.0 B1 and then 4.0 B2, and finally 4.0 RC, I can confidently say that these improvements will make your job as a workflow developer much easier.

How to Use This Book

An ancient proverb says, "Tell me and I'll forget; show me and I may not remember; involve me and I'll understand." Based on this truth, this book presents a series of workflow projects; starting with simple solutions and gradually increasing in complexity. New concepts are introduced in each chapter. In each project, I'll show you step-by-step how to implement them for yourself. I recommend that you work through each chapter in order because each chapter builds on both concepts and code that was developed in previous chapters.

As an alternative, you can download the final implementation of each chapter from www.apress.com. You can then read the book and follow along with the downloaded code. This approach is recommended for more experienced developers who are looking for a quick tutorial or perhaps an explanation of specific concepts.

In either case, once you have read the book and are starting to implement workflow in your own solutions, the sample projects provided in this book make a handy reference guide. A topical reference is provided to help you find the appropriate chapters to look at for each of the WF concepts.

Several of the projects require a SQL Server database. Just about any version will work, including the Microsoft Data Engine (MSDE) provided with Visual Studio. You will need to create the databases and configure the appropriate connection strings. You can download the database scripts from www.apress.com, which provide everything you'll need to create the schemas.

Chapter Outline

This book's projects (chapters) are grouped into five sections. In many cases, the same solution is provided in all chapters in that section, with each chapter providing new features to the project from the previous chapter.

Section 1: Basic Concepts

In the first section, you'll build three simple workflows. In Chapter 1, you'll create a workflow using the workflow designer and some of the basic built-in activities. In Chapter 2, you'll re-create the same workflow in code. This will give you an opportunity early on to see both designer workflows and coded workflows. Both types will be demonstrated throughout the book. In Chapter 3, you'll use the flowchart activity, which provides the ultimate flexibility in designing complex workflows.

Section 2: Designing Workflows

In the second section, you'll build a workflow that computes the cost of an order. Each chapter will add additional features to the project from the previous chapter. The project in Chapter 4 demonstrates how to pass data into and out of a workflow. In Chapter 5, you'll interactively execute activities based on a collection of objects. Chapter 6 will show you how to handle and throw exceptions. In Chapter 7, you'll explore the two main ways to extend the workflow activities: creating a custom activity and executing the InvokeMethod activity.

Section 3: Communication

In the third section, you'll build workflows that take advantage of the integration with the Windows Communication Foundation (WCF). The project in Chapter 8 builds a console application that communicates with other instances of the same application using WCF messages. In Chapter 9, the console app is replaced with a Windows Presentation Foundation (WPF) application, which demonstrates how the application and workflow can interact with each other. In Chapter 10, you'll host a workflow in a WCF web service. You'll also consume that service using a workflow application.

Section 4: Workflow Extensions

A key component of workflow design is the use of extensions to configure the environment in which the workflow activities operate. The project in Chapter 11, for instance, demonstrates how to use the standard SQL persistence extension. This extension allows the state of the workflow to be written to a SQL database and retrieved later, when the workflow is resumed. In Chapter 12, you'll explore ways to extend and customize the persistence operation. The project in Chapter 13 demonstrates how to track the execution of a workflow in a variety of ways. In Chapter 14, you'll use database transactions to ensure data consistency across multiple activities. In Chapter 15, you'll execute the application updates on the same database transaction used to persist the workflow state. This will guarantee that the workflow state and application data stay consistent. Finally, in Chapter 16, you'll learn how to configure extensions when the workflow is instantiated by a WorkflowServiceHost.

Section 5: Advanced Topics

Chapter 17 demonstrates how to include logic within the workflow design to handle abnormal conditions such as compensation and cancellation. In Chapter 18, you'll see how to use both built-in and custom activities to support collections of objects. The project in Chapter 19 uses the `Interop` activity to execute workflows and activities that were created using previous versions of WF. In Chapter 20, you'll use the `Policy` activity from version 3.0 in a WF 4.0 workflow.

Appendix

The Appendix describes a sample workflow that demonstrates many of the concepts presented in this book. It is designed as a review of the key concepts while providing another example of a workflow implementation. This project is not described in a step-by-step fashion. Instead, the final code can be downloaded from `www.apress.com`.

■ ■ ■

PART 1

Introduction

The Workflow Foundation included in .Net 4.0 (referred to as WF 4.0) represents a whole new paradigm for building workflow-based applications. It has been completely re-engineered from the ground up. In this section, you'll design some simple workflows and learn the basic concepts. In subsequent sections, you'll develop more complex solutions as you explore the capabilities provided by WF 4.0.

CHAPTER 1

Building a Simple Workflow

Let's start by building a simple workflow. Start Visual Studio (VS) 2010 and select the New Project link. Under the Installed Templates, navigate to Visual C#, Workflow and you should see that four templates have been provided. Select the Workflow Console Application, as shown in Figure 1-1. Enter the name as **Chapter01** and select a suitable location for this solution.

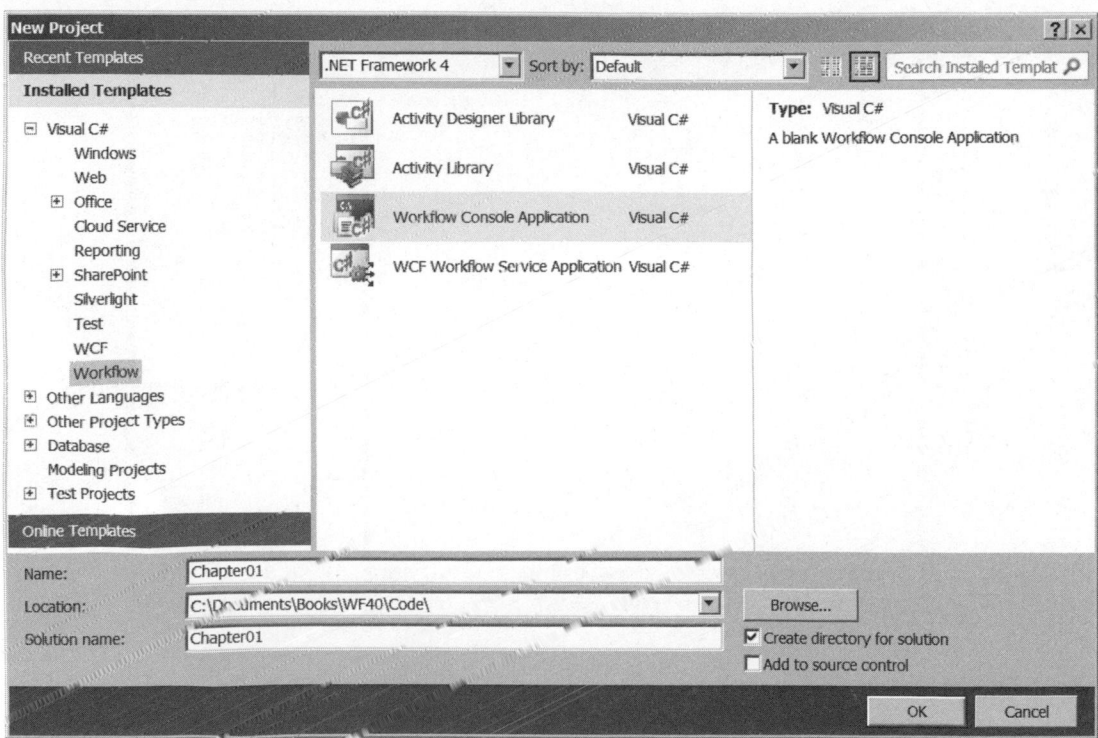

Figure 1-1. *Creating a new workflow project*

A Simple Workflow

The template generates a `Program.cs` file, which implements the console application. It also generates a `Workflow1.xaml` file, which defines the activities in your workflow. If you've worked with Windows Presentation Framework (WPF) applications, you're probably familiar with xaml, which is an XML-like syntax used for declaring programmatic elements. Instead of labels, text boxes, and grids, however, this file will contain the activity-derived elements in your workflow definition. VS 2010 provides a designer that allows you to graphically view and edit these activities.

Exploring the IDE

Figure 1-2 shows a typical layout of the Visual Studio 2010 integrated development environment (IDE). The Toolbox on the left contains the built-in and custom activities that are available to you. I have expanded some of the more common groups of activities. The Solution Explorer and the Properties window are on the right. The bottom window contains a number of tabs including the Error List and Output window.

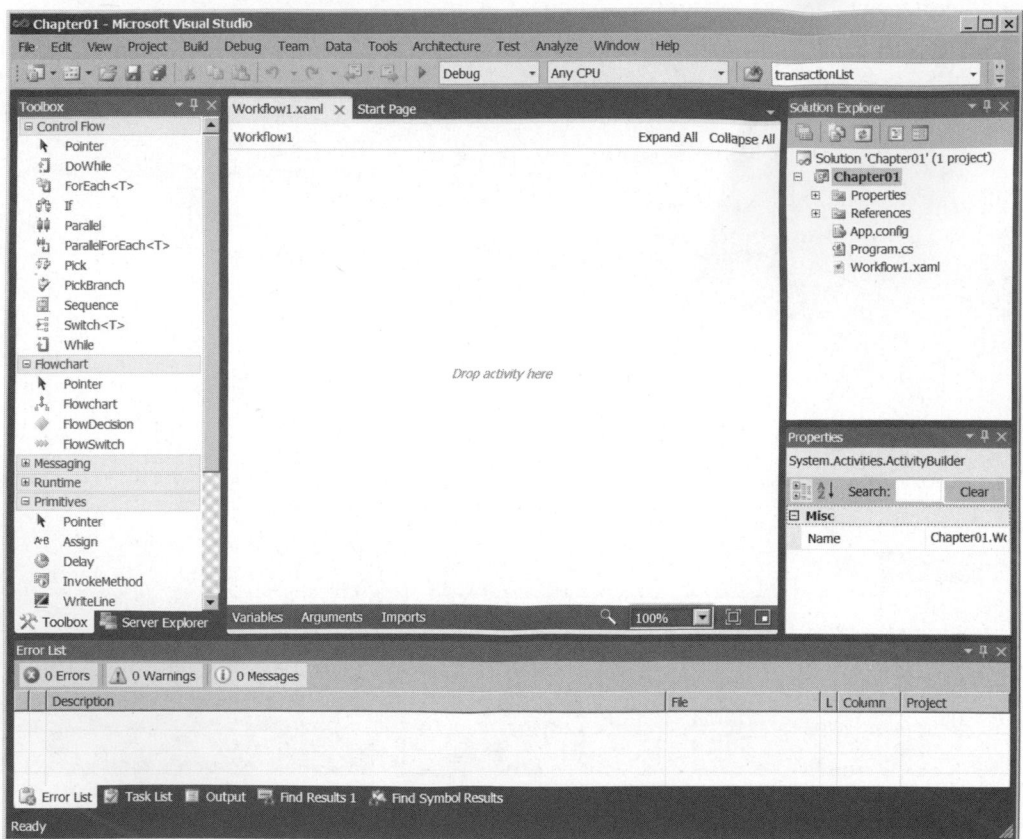

Figure 1-2. Typical Visual Studio 2010 IDE

The WF 4.0 designer is in the middle. At the bottom right, there are controls for zooming. Workflow designs in version 4.0 tend to be somewhat long, and this is a handy feature to see the "big picture" or to find a particular activity. There are three controls at the bottom left for displaying the variables, arguments, and imported assemblies. When you click the Variables control, a window appears to show the existing variables, as shown in Figure 1-3. To close this window, click the Variables control again.

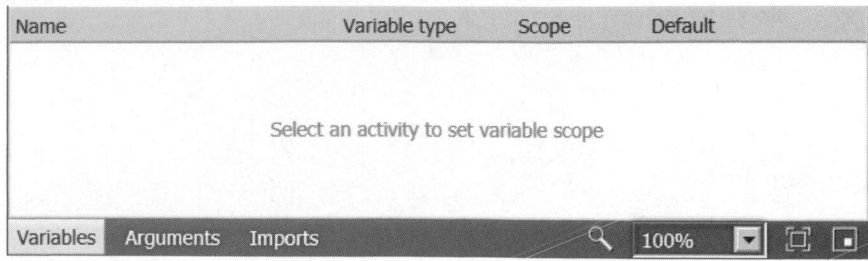

Figure 1-3. *Viewing workflow variables*

If you think of your workflow as a class, variables are the class members. You can use them to store data that must be shared between activities. You can define the scope of a variable—either the entire workflow or just a specific activity (and its children). Arguments are similar to variables, but they are intended for passing data in or out of the workflow. You can think of them as method parameters.

Figure 1-4 shows what the Arguments window looks like. Notice the Direction column; it defines whether the data is passed in to the workflow or sent out of the workflow.

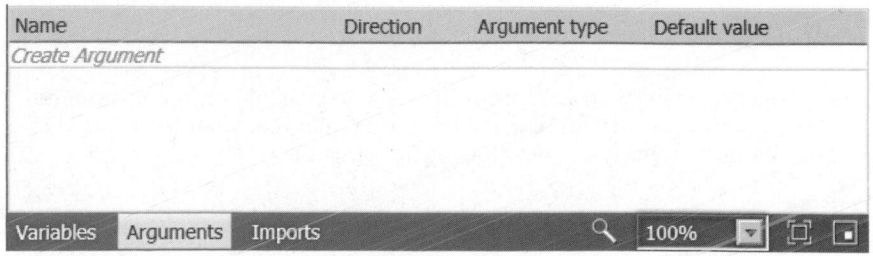

Figure 1-4. *Viewing workflow arguments*

Designing the Workflow

The initial workflow designer is empty. You will drag activities onto it to define the workflow behavior. This project will initially just display the greeting "Hello, World!" Later, you'll embellish it somewhat to discover some of the procedural activities. To start, drag a Sequence activity onto the designer. Then drag a WriteLine activity to the Sequence. The diagram should look like the one shown in Figure 1-5.

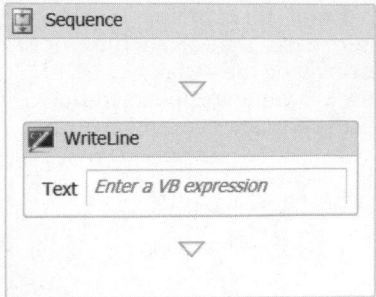

Figure 1-5. *Adding a WriteLine activity*

The Properties window is shown in Figure 1-6.

System.Activities.Statements.WriteLine		
⊞ ↓ Search:		Clear
⊟ **Misc**		
DisplayName	WriteLine	
Text	*Enter a VB expression*	...
TextWriter	*Enter a VB expression*	...

Figure 1-6. *WriteLine Properties window*

The `DisplayName` property is the text shown in the diagram. You should give this a more meaningful name because when you have many `WriteLine` activities, it will help you remember what this is for. Change this to **Hello**. Also, enter the `Text` property as the following literal string:

```
"Hello, World!"
```

The `Text` property can be any expression that results in a string. You can click the ellipses, which will display a dialog in which you can enter an expression.

You can leave the `TextWriter` property blank. By default, the text will be written to the console. You can specify a class derived from `TextWriter` (new for .Net 4.0) if you want to specify a different implementation. This will be demonstrated in Chapter 9.

Reviewing Program.cs

Open the `Program.cs` file, which will implement the console application and launch the workflow. The default implementation generated by the template is shown in Listing 1-1.

Listing 1-1. *Default Program.cs Implementation*

```
using System;
```

```
using System.Linq;
using System.Activities;
using System.Activities.Statements;

namespace Chapter01
{

    class Program
    {
        static void Main(string[] args)
        {
            WorkflowInvoker.Invoke(new Workflow1());

            Console.WriteLine("Press ENTER to exit");
            Console.ReadLine();
        }
    }
}
```

The static `WorkflowInvoker` class is used to start the workflow that is defined by the `Workflow1` class. The lines in bold are not in the default implementation:

```
Console.WriteLine("Press ENTER to exit");
Console.ReadLine();
```

I added these lines so the console app does not exit before you have a chance to see the output. You should add this code to your project.

Running the Application

Now press F5 to run the application. The result should look like this:

```
Hello, World!
Press ENTER to exit
```

Adding Procedural Elements

WF 4.0 provides a number of procedural elements such as `If`, `While`, `Assign`, `Sequence`, and so on. To demonstrate how they work, you'll enhance this greeting. First, like some old-fashioned clocks, you'll sound a number of bells to indicate the time (one bell for each hour). Open the `Workflow1.asmx` file.

Using Variables

With WF 4.0, you must declare all variables that are used by the workflow elements. You'll need two variables: one to indicate how many bells are needed and another to serve as a counter to keep track of how many bells have been sounded so far. Click the Variables button. If the Variables window looks like the one shown in Figure 1-3 (there are no variables and no way to add a variable), it means that no scope has been defined.

Click the main Sequence activity, and the Variables window should look like the one shown in Figure 1-7.

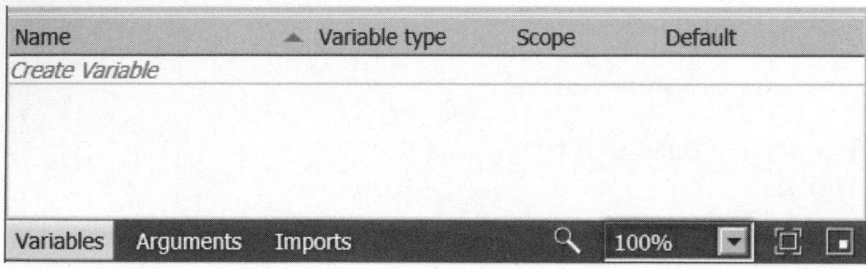

Figure 1-7. *Variable window with a defined scope*

Click the *Create Variable* link. Enter the name as **counter** and select Int32 as the variable type. You can leave the scope as Sequence. This means that the variable is available to the Sequence activity and all its descendants. Enter the Default as **1**. The Variables window should now look like the one shown in Figure 1-8.

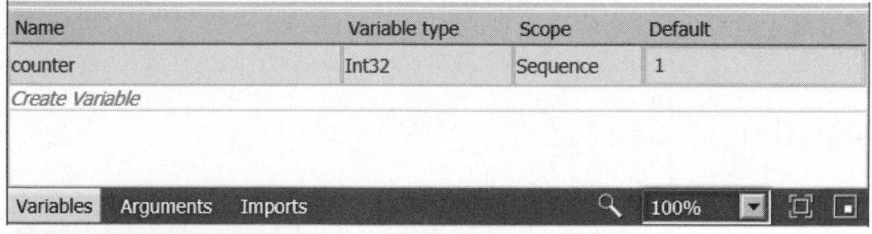

Figure 1-8. *Variable window with a new variable*

The Properties window also has these same values (see Figure 1-9). You can enter the variable's properties in the Properties window or the Variables window.

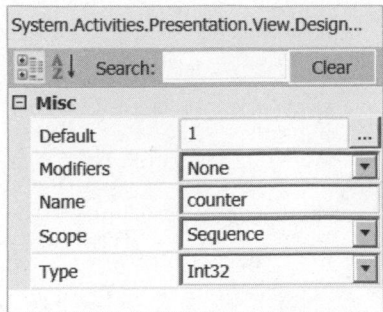

Figure 1-9. Properties window of a selected variable

Click the *Create Variable* link again. This time, use the Properties window to enter the properties. Enter the Name as **numberBells** and the Type as **Int32**. Leave the Scope as Sequence. For the Default property, click the ellipses, which will display the Expression editor, as shown in Figure 1-10.

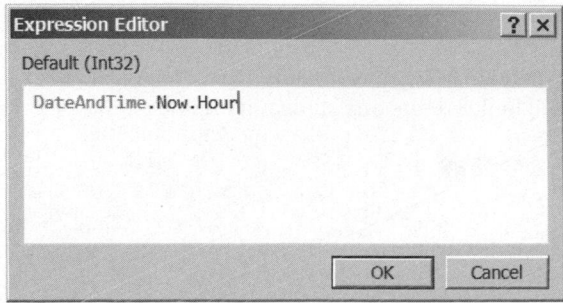

Figure 1-10. Expression editor

■ **Tip** One of the things you'll notice about WF 4.0 is that it relies a lot on expressions. Many properties can be defined using an expression. However, the form doesn't usually leave enough room to write complex expressions. To solve this, the expression editor can be used by clicking the ellipses next to any field that uses an expression. Expressions can use variables, arguments, and system functions just as you would in code.

Enter the expression DateAndTime.Now.Hour for the Default property. This will set the numberBells variable to the current hour of the day. The Variables window should now look like the one shown in Figure 1-11.

Name	Variable type	Scope	Default
counter	Int32	Sequence	1
numberBells	Int32	Sequence	DateAndTime.Now.Hour
Create Variable			

Variables   Arguments   Imports   🔍 100%

Figure 1-11. *Completed Variables window*

If

The Hour member of the DateAndTime class returns the hour based on a 24-hour clock. For example, for 2 PM, it will return 14. So you'll need to adjust for this because you should ring 2 bells, not 14. In code, you would write this as follows:

```
if (numberBells > 12)
    numberBells -= 12;
```

However, in WF 4.0, you'll need to use an If and an Assign activity to accomplish this. Drag an If activity just below the Hello activity. The diagram should look like the one shown in Figure 1-12.

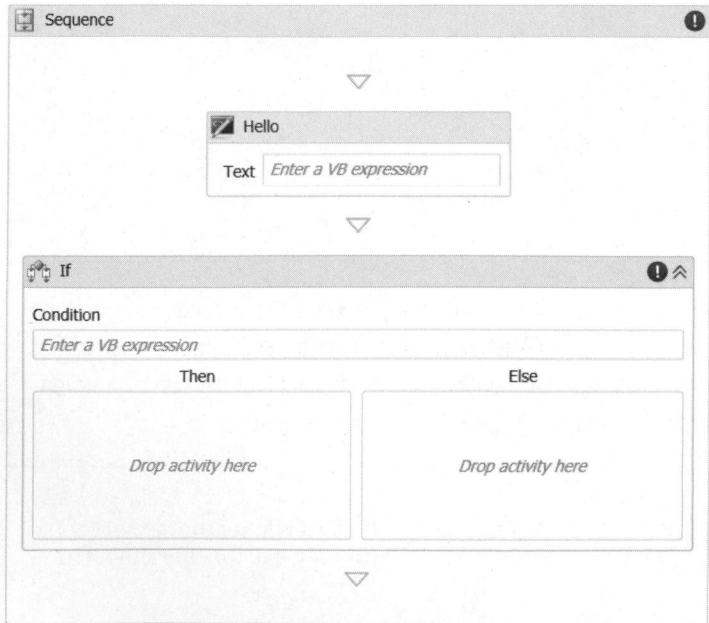

Figure 1-12. *Adding an If activity*

■ **Tip** Notice the red error circles on the diagram. If you hover the mouse over them, they will display the associated warning/error. The error on the If activity lets you know that you haven't specified the Condition property. The warning on the Sequence activity simply indicates that one or more child activities have an error.

In the Properties window, change the DisplayName to **Adjust for PM**. The If activity consists of three elements. The Condition specifies the logic that is evaluated. It should resolve to a Boolean (true or false) value. Then contains the activities that are executed when the Condition is true, and Else contains the activities that are executed when the Condition is false. You do not have to specify both Then and Else; only one is required. If no activity is defined, then no activities are executed. Enter the Condition as **numberBells > 12**.

Assign

Drag an Assign activity to the Then section. The Assign activity allows you to assign a value to a variable or an argument. The activity should look like the one shown in Figure 1-13.

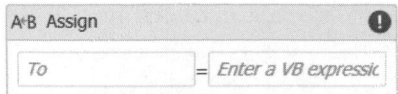

Figure 1-13. *Defining an Assign activity*

Both the To and Value properties accept an expression. You can either enter the expression directly in the box provided or click the ellipses to use the Expression editor. For the To property, enter **numberBells**. For the Value property, enter **numberBells – 12**. The Properties window should look like the one shown in Figure 1-14.

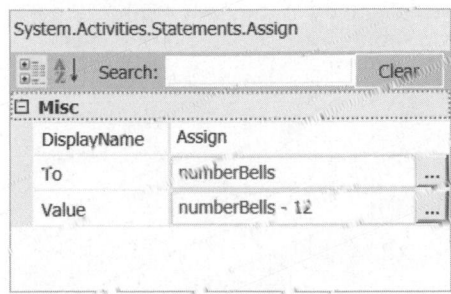

Figure 1-14. *Assign activity Properties window*

Many activities are *compound activities*, meaning that they can contain other activities. The If activity is a good example of this. As you design more complex workflows, you will be navigating through several layers in the workflow design.

While

Now you'll add a `While` activity to sound the bells. Drag a `While` activity just below "Adjust for PM". Set the `DisplayName` to **Sound Bells**. The diagram should look like the one shown in Figure 1-15.

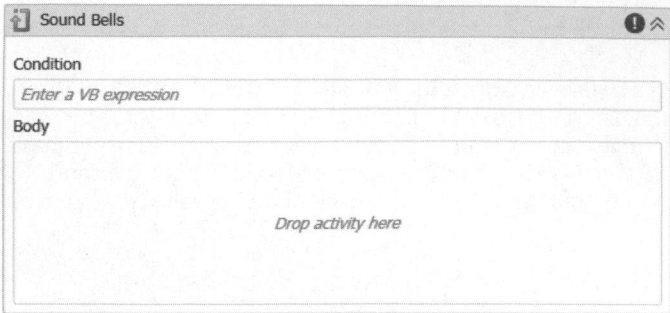

Figure 1-15. *Defining a While activity*

In a `While` activity, the activity in the Body section is executed as long as the Condition is `true`. The Condition is evaluated first and then, if `true`, the activities are executed. This is repeated until the Condition is `false`.

■ **Note** The `DoWhile` activity is identical to `While`, except that the activities are executed first and then the Condition is evaluated. This ensures that the activities are executed at least once. With a `While` activity, if the Condition is initially `false`, the activities in the Body section will never be executed.

Enter the Condition as **counter <= numberBells**. Drag a Sequence activity to the Body section. Set the `DisplayName` of the Sequence activity to **Sound Bell**. The diagram should look like the one shown in Figure 1-16.

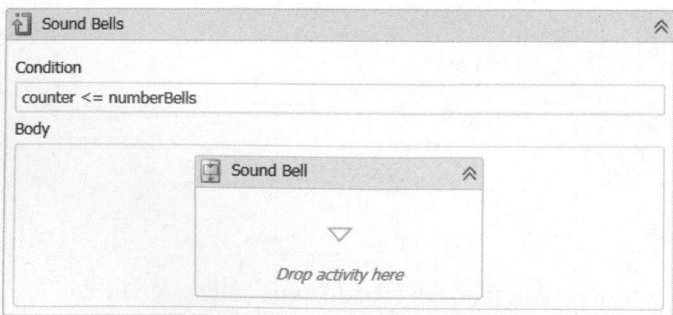

Figure 1-16. *A While activity that contains a sequence*

Sequence

You'll drag three activities onto the "Sound Bell" Sequence. In this exercise, you won't actually sound a bell. Instead, you will write a line of text to the console that will count the bells (as if they were actually sounding). Drag a WriteLine activity to the "Sound Bell" activity. In the Text property, enter the following:

```
counter.ToString()
```

This will display the current value of the counter to the console. Then drag an Assign activity just below the WriteLine activity. For the To property, enter **counter**; in the Value property, enter **counter + 1**. This simply increments the counter.

Delay

Finally, drag a Delay activity just below the Assign activity. A Delay activity pauses a workflow for a specified period of time. The only property of a Delay activity is the Duration, which indicates how long to pause. This should be specified as a TimeSpan class. Enter the following expression:

```
TimeSpan.FromSeconds(1)
```

The diagram should look like the one shown in Figure 1-17.

Figure 1-17. *Completed sequence diagram*

More Embellishments

Click the Collapse link on the top-right corner of the "Sound Bells" While activity. The workflow diagram should look like the one shown in Figure 1-18.

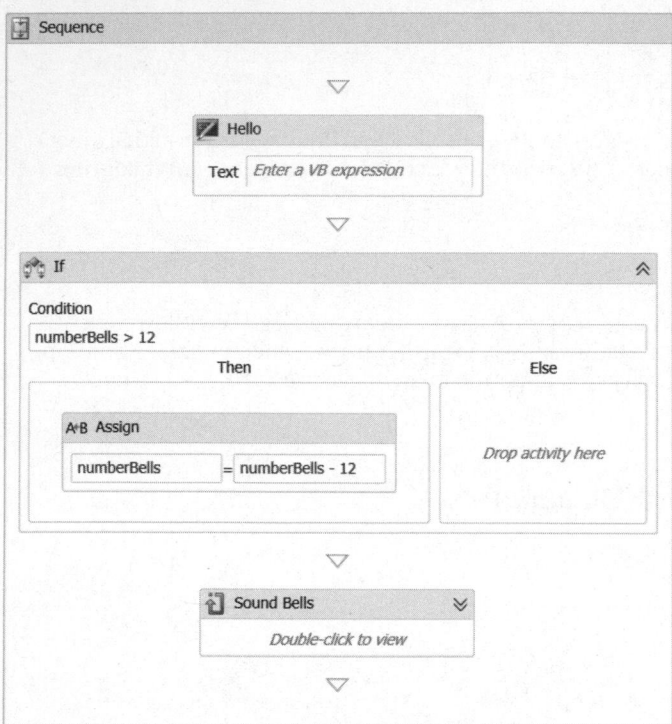

Figure 1-18. *Collapsed While activity*

Drag a `WriteLine` activity just below the `Sound Bells` activity. Change the `DisplayName` to **Display Time**; for the `Text` property, enter the following expression:

```
"The time is: " + DateAndTime.Now.ToString()
```

Drag an `If` activity just below "Display Time" and set the `DisplayName` to **Greeting**. For the `Condition`, enter the following expression:

```
DateAndTime.Now.Hour >= 18
```

Drag a `WriteLine` activity to both the Then and Else sections. For the Then section, enter the Text as **"Good Evening"**; for the Else section, enter the Text as **"Good Day"**. The "Greeting" activity should look like the one shown in Figure 1-19.

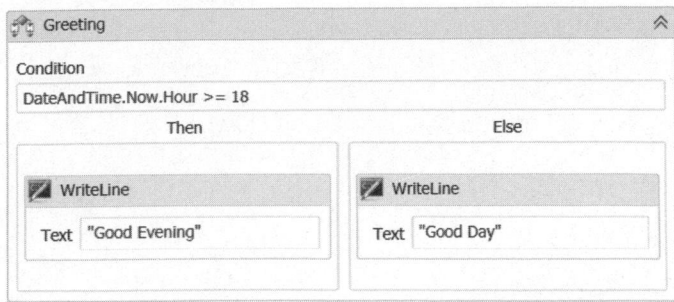

Figure 1-19. *Greeting activity*

Running the Application

Press F5 to run the application. Depending on the time of day, your results will be similar to this:

```
Hello, World!
1
2
The time is: 10/28/2009 2:26:02 PM
Good Day
Press ENTER to exit
```

Navigating the Designer

Even with this fairly simple workflow, you can see that it will be difficult to display the entire diagram. Fortunately, the designer has some useful features to help you work on large workflows. At the top-right corner of the designer, click the Collapse All link. The diagram should look similar to the one shown in Figure 1-20.

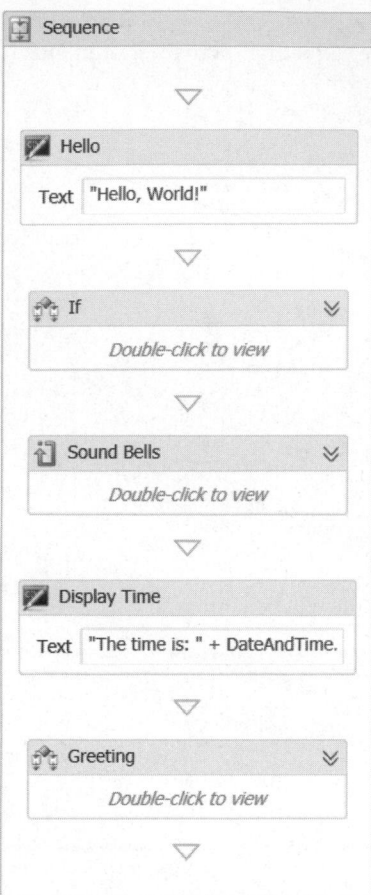

Figure 1-20. *Collapsed workflow diagram*

This gives you a quick way to see the top-level activities. Now click the Expand All link. This expands all the activities, but now you can see only part of the diagram. Click the Overview control at the bottom-right corner of the designer, which displays a window that shows the entire diagram. The yellow box indicates the viewable area. You can drag this around, which will pan the main window to the desired area. Close the overview window and click the Fit to screen control. This will zoom in as far as possible and still keep the entire diagram visible. Depending on your monitor size, this may be a little difficult to read. The drop-down control will allow you to change the zoom level. Finally, if you click the magnifying class, the zoom will return to the default 100 percent level.

Double-click the "Sound Bell" activity. This will display only that activity (and its child activities). To help you know where you are in the overall workflow, a navigation bar is displayed like the one shown in Figure 1-21.

Workflow1 > Sequence > Sound Bells > Sound Bell

Figure 1-21. Designer navigation bar

You can click any of the links on this navigation bar to display that level within the workflow design. Click the Workflow1 link to display the top-level workflow.

Looking a Bit Deeper

Let's take a brief look at what you just implemented. First, I mentioned earlier that the workflow was defined by an .xaml file. So far, you have been using the designer to graphically define the workflow. Now you'll see what the designer actually generated for that design. In the Solution Explorer, right-click the Sequence1.xaml file and choose Code View. You might get a warning that the file is already open. Just click Yes to let it close the existing designer window. The .xaml code is shown in Listing 1-2.

Listing 1-2. Sequence1.xaml source code

```
<p:Activity mc:Ignorable="" x:Class="Chapter01.Sequence1"
  xmlns="http://schemas.microsoft.com/netfx/2009/xaml/activities/design"
  xmlns:__Sequence1="clr-namespace:Chapter01;"
  xmlns:mc="http://schemas.openxmlformats.org/markup-compatibility/2006"
  xmlns:p="http://schemas.microsoft.com/netfx/2009/xaml/activities"
  xmlns:sad="clr-namespace:System.Activities.Debugger;assembly=System.Activities"
  xmlns:x="http://schemas.microsoft.com/winfx/2006/xaml">
  <p:Sequence sad:XamlDebuggerXmlReader.FileName=
    "C:\Documents\Books\WF40\Code\Chapter01\Chapter01\Sequence1.xaml">
<p:Sequence.Variables>
      <p:Variable x:TypeArguments="x:Int32" Default="[1]" Name="counter" />
      <p:Variable x:TypeArguments="x:Int32" Default="[DateTime.Now.Hour]"
        Name="numberBells" />
    </p:Sequence.Variables>
<p:WriteLine DisplayName="Hello">["Hello, World!"]</p:WriteLine>
<p:If Condition="[numberBells &gt; 12]" DisplayName="Adjust for PM">
      <p:If.Then>
        <p:Assign>
          <p:Assign.To>
            <p:OutArgument x:TypeArguments="x:Int32">[numberBells]</p:OutArgument>
          </p:Assign.To>
          <p:Assign.Value>
            <p:InArgument x:TypeArguments="x:Int32">[numberBells - 12]
              </p:InArgument>
          </p:Assign.Value>
        </p:Assign>
```

```xml
      </p:If.Then>
    </p:If>
<p:While Condition="[counter &lt;= numberBells]" DisplayName="Sound Bells">
      <p:Sequence DisplayName="Sound Bell">
        <p:WriteLine>[counter.ToString()]</p:WriteLine>
        <p:Assign>
          <p:Assign.To>
            <p:OutArgument x:TypeArguments="x:Int32">[counter]</p:OutArgument>
          </p:Assign.To>
          <p:Assign.Value>
            <p:InArgument x:TypeArguments="x:Int32">[counter + 1]</p:InArgument>
          </p:Assign.Value>
        </p:Assign>
        <p:Delay>[TimeSpan.FromSeconds(1)]</p:Delay>
      </p:Sequence>
    </p:While>
<p:WriteLine DisplayName="Display Time">
      ["The time is: " + DateTime.Now.ToString()]</p:WriteLine>
<p:If Condition="[DateTime.Now.Hour &gt;= 18]" DisplayName="Greeting">
      <p:If.Else>
        <p:WriteLine>["Good Day"]</p:WriteLine>
      </p:If.Else>
      <p:If.Then>
        <p:WriteLine>["Good Evening"]</p:WriteLine>
      </p:If.Then>
    </p:If>
  </p:Sequence>
</p:Activity>

<Activity mc:Ignorable="sap" x:Class="Chapter01.Workflow1"
  mva:VisualBasic.Settings=
    "Assembly references and imported namespaces serialized as XML namespaces"
  xmlns="http://schemas.microsoft.com/netfx/2009/xaml/activities"
  xmlns:mc="http://schemas.openxmlformats.org/markup-compatibility/2006"
  xmlns:mv="clr-namespace:Microsoft.VisualBasic;assembly=Microsoft.VisualBasic,
    Version=10.0.0.0, Culture=neutral, PublicKeyToken=b03f5f7f11d50a3a"
  xmlns:mv1="clr-namespace:Microsoft.VisualBasic;assembly=System"
  xmlns:mva="clr-namespace:Microsoft.VisualBasic.Activities;
    assembly=System.Activities"
  xmlns:s="clr-namespace:System;assembly=mscorlib, Version=4.0.0.0,
    Culture=neutral, PublicKeyToken=b77a5c561934e089"
  xmlns:s1="clr-namespace:System;assembly=mscorlib"
  xmlns:s2="clr-namespace:System;assembly=System"
```

```
    xmlns:s3="clr-namespace:System;assembly=System.Xml"
    xmlns:s4="clr-namespace:System;assembly=System.Core"
    xmlns:sa="clr-namespace:System.Activities;assembly=System.Activities,
      Version=4.0.0.0, Culture=neutral, PublicKeyToken=31bf3856ad364e35"
    xmlns:sad="clr-namespace:System.Activities.Debugger;assembly=System.Activities"
    xmlns:sap="http://schemas.microsoft.com/netfx/2009/xaml/activities/presentation"
    xmlns:scg="clr-namespace:System.Collections.Generic;assembly=System"
    xmlns:scg1="clr-namespace:System.Collections.Generic;
      assembly=System.ServiceModel"
    xmlns:scg2="clr-namespace:System.Collections.Generic;assembly=System.Core"
    xmlns:scg3="clr-namespace:System.Collections.Generic;assembly=mscorlib"
    xmlns:sd="clr-namespace:System.Data;assembly=System.Data"
    xmlns:sd1="clr-namespace:System.Data;assembly=System.Data.DataSetExtensions"
    xmlns:sl="clr-namespace:System.Linq;assembly=System.Core"
    xmlns:st="clr-namespace:System.Text;assembly=mscorlib"
    xmlns:x="http://schemas.microsoft.com/winfx/2006/xaml">
    <sap:WorkflowViewStateService.ViewState>
      <scg3:Dictionary x:TypeArguments="x:String, x:Object">
        <x:Boolean x:Key="ShouldExpandAll">False</x:Boolean>
        <x:Boolean x:Key="ShouldCollapseAll">True</x:Boolean>
      </scg3:Dictionary>
    </sap:WorkflowViewStateService.ViewState>
    <Sequence sad:XamlDebuggerXmlReader.FileName=
      "C:\Documents\Books\WF40\Code\Chapter01\Chapter01\Workflow1.xaml"
      sap:VirtualizedContainerService.HintSize="233.6,552">
<Sequence.Variables>
        <Variable x:TypeArguments="x:Int32" Default="1" Name="counter" />
        <Variable x:TypeArguments="x:Int32" Default="[DateAndTime.Now.Hour]"
          Name="numberBells" />
      </Sequence.Variables>
      <sap:WorkflowViewStateService.ViewState>
        <scg3:Dictionary x:TypeArguments="x:String, x:Object">
          <x:Boolean x:Key="IsExpanded">True</x:Boolean>
        </scg3:Dictionary>
      </sap:WorkflowViewStateService.ViewState>
<WriteLine DisplayName="Hello"
        sap:VirtualizedContainerService.HintSize="211.2,59.2"
        Text="Hello, World!" />
<If Condition="[numberBells &gt; 12]"
        sap:VirtualizedContainerService.HintSize="211.2,49.6">
        <sap:WorkflowViewStateService.ViewState>
          <scg3:Dictionary x:TypeArguments="x:String, x:Object">
            <x:Boolean x:Key="IsExpanded">True</x:Boolean>
```

```xml
            <x:Boolean x:Key="IsPinned">False</x:Boolean>
          </scg3:Dictionary>
        </sap:WorkflowViewStateService.ViewState>
      <If.Then>
        <Assign sap:VirtualizedContainerService.HintSize="289.6,100.8">
          <Assign.To>
            <OutArgument x:TypeArguments="x:Int32">[numberBells]</OutArgument>
          </Assign.To>
          <Assign.Value>
            <InArgument x:TypeArguments="x:Int32">[numberBells - 12]</InArgument>
          </Assign.Value>
        </Assign>
      </If.Then>
    </If>
<While DisplayName="Sound Bells"
      sap:VirtualizedContainerService.HintSize="211.2,49.6">
      <sap:WorkflowViewStateService.ViewState>
        <scg3:Dictionary x:TypeArguments="x:String, x:Object">
          <x:Boolean x:Key="IsExpanded">False</x:Boolean>
          <x:Boolean x:Key="IsPinned">False</x:Boolean>
        </scg3:Dictionary>
      </sap:WorkflowViewStateService.ViewState>
      <While.Condition>[counter &lt;= numberBells]</While.Condition>
      <Sequence DisplayName="Sound Bell"
        sap:VirtualizedContainerService.HintSize="438.4,100.8">
        <sap:WorkflowViewStateService.ViewState>
          <scg3:Dictionary x:TypeArguments="x:String, x:Object">
            <x:Boolean x:Key="IsExpanded">True</x:Boolean>
          </scg3:Dictionary>
        </sap:WorkflowViewStateService.ViewState>
        <WriteLine sap:VirtualizedContainerService.HintSize="243.2,59.2"
          Text="[counter.ToString()]" />
        <Assign sap:VirtualizedContainerService.HintSize="243.2,57.6">
          <Assign.To>
            <OutArgument x:TypeArguments="x:Int32">[counter]</OutArgument>
          </Assign.To>
          <Assign.Value>
            <InArgument x:TypeArguments="x:Int32">[counter + 1]</InArgument>
          </Assign.Value>
        </Assign>
        <Delay Duration="[TimeSpan.FromSeconds(1)]"
          sap:VirtualizedContainerService.HintSize="243.2,22.4" />
      </Sequence>
```

```
      </While>
<WriteLine DisplayName="Display Time"
         sap:VirtualizedContainerService.HintSize="211.2,59.2"
         Text="[&quot;The time is: &quot; + DateAndTime.Now.ToString()]" />
<If Condition="[DateAndTime.Now.Hour &gt;= 18]" DisplayName="Greeting"
         sap:VirtualizedContainerService.HintSize="211.2,49.6">
         <sap:WorkflowViewStateService.ViewState>
           <scg3:Dictionary x:TypeArguments="x:String, x:Object">
             <x:Boolean x:Key="IsExpanded">False</x:Boolean>
             <x:Boolean x:Key="IsPinned">False</x:Boolean>
           </scg3:Dictionary>
         </sap:WorkflowViewStateService.ViewState>
         <If.Then>
           <WriteLine sap:VirtualizedContainerService.HintSize="219.2,100.8"
             Text="Good Evening" />
         </If.Then>
         <If.Else>
           <WriteLine sap:VirtualizedContainerService.HintSize="219.2,100.8"
             Text="Good Day" />
         </If.Else>
      </If>
    </Sequence>
</Activity>
```

I made some lines bold to help you find the top-level activities. First, the `Variables` section defines the two variables you created. Then there's a `WriteLine` activity named "Hello" and an `If` activity named "Adjust for PM". This is followed by a `While` activity named "Sound Bells", a `WriteLine` activity named "Display Time", and an `If` activity named "Greeting".

One key point that I want you to see is that there is no executable code here. This file is just a nested collection of properties. For example, to increment the counter, you would normally expect to see a line of code like this:

```
counter = counter + 1;
```

Instead you have an `Assign` class with a `counter` expression and a `counter + 1` expression. The actual execution that makes the assignment of `counter = counter + 1` is performed by the `Assign` activity. Code is executed only in the `Activity` classes, and there is no code execution in the workflow definition.

Differences from Previous Versions

If you have used previous versions of Workflow Foundation (version 3.0 or 3.5), you might be wondering what happened here. WF 4.0 is a complete departure from previous versions of Workflow. Your previous Workflow applications will run just fine under .Net 4.0 because the previous set of activities and services were carried forward with minimal changes. WF 4.0, however, is a completely new design. The activities and services from WF 4.0 are not interchangeable with previous versions. So you can design, implement, and maintain workflows using the WF 3.5 approach. Or you can choose to use the WF 4.0 paradigm; either will work fine. But you cannot switch back and forth, except for a few scenarios that are described later in this book.

In WF 3.5, there was a code class and a designer class. The code class contained the implementation for the CodeActivity objects. It also contained the definition of the class members and the event handler code. In WF 4.0, there is no code class. Probably the most notable effect of this is that there is no CodeActivity object in WF 4.0. To compensate for this, WF 4.0 provides activities to accomplish some of the common tasks previously performed by CodeActivity objects. WriteLine and Assign are two such activities. If the built-in activities are not sufficient, you can create a custom activity to perform the task you would have used a CodeActivity for.

Another key difference is the explicit use of variables and arguments. Again, because there is no code file, you can't simply add class members as you would with normal class development. Instead, you have to define these using the "Workflow way."

Finally, you may have noticed when looking at the Program.cs file that there is no WorkflowRuntime class. Previously, you would have created the WorkflowRuntime class and then called its CreateWorkflow() method. With WF 4.0, the code simply calls this:

```
WorkflowInvoker.Invoke(new Workflow1());
```

Throughout this document, you will undoubtedly notice other differences. For example, there is no longer a state machine workflow. I won't point these out because the purpose of this book is not to illustrate the differences. However, I did want to note some of the obvious changes just in case, like me, you had to scratch your head for a few minutes when looking at WF 4.0 for the first time.

CHAPTER 2

■ ■ ■

Coded Workflows

In Chapter 1, you implemented a fairly simple workflow using the workflow designer. Now you'll implement the same workflow using code instead. Any workflow can be implemented in code or with the designer; the choice is simply a matter of preference. However, implementing a workflow in code will help you gain a better sense of how workflow works.

Creating a Console Application

To start, create a simple console application (do not use a workflow template), as shown in Figure 2-1.

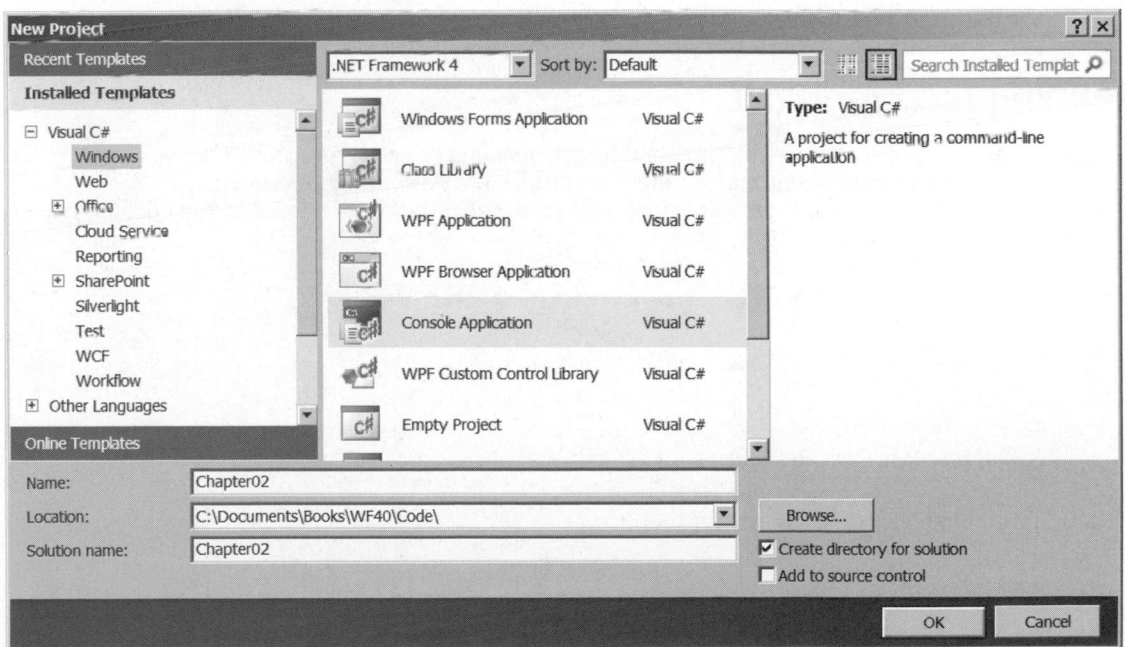

Figure 2-1. *Creating a console application*

Add a reference to System.Activities. This will enable you to use the workflow activities in your application. Then replace the set of namespaces in your Program.cs file with the following:

```
using System;
using System.Activities;
using System.Activities.Statements;
using System.Activities.Expressions;
```

To implement the main() function, enter the following code:

```
WorkflowInvoker.Invoke(CreateWorkflow());

Console.WriteLine("Press ENTER to exit");
Console.ReadLine();
```

Note that this is identical to the main() implementation from Chapter 1. If you want, you can simply copy and paste from your previous application. There is one difference, however. The following line calls CreateWorkflow() instead of new Workflow1():

```
WorkflowInvoker.Invoke(CreateWorkflow());
```

Workflow1 was defined in the Workflow1.xaml file, which was generated by the workflow designer. CreateWorkflow() is a method that you'll implement now.

Defining the Workflow

As I mentioned in the last chapter, a *workflow* is just a collection of nested properties. To be more accurate, it is a collection of nested classes and their properties. To simplify this process, I'll show you the implementation to enter, one level at a time. I'll explain what the code is doing as you go. Start by adding the following method to the Program.cs file:

```
static Activity CreateWorkflow()
{
    Variable<int> numberBells = new Variable<int>()
    {
        Name = "numberBells",
        Default = DateTime.Now.Hour
    };
    Variable<int> counter = new Variable<int>()
    {
        Name = "counter",
        Default = 1
    };
```

```
    return new Sequence()
    {
    };
}
```

The `CreateWorkflow()` method first creates two `Variable<T>` template classes of type int, called `numberBells` and `counter`. These are the variables used by the various activities.

The `CreateWorkflow()` method is declared to return an `Activity`, which is what the `WorkflowInvoker` class is expecting. It actually returns an anonymous instance of the Sequence class. The `Activity` class is the base class from which all workflow activities are derived, including Sequence. So the compiler returns the Sequence instance as its base class, `Activity`.

Implementing Level 1

So far, you have defined an empty Sequence activity. This is roughly equivalent to creating a new workflow that has a Sequence with no activities. Now, define the activities on this Sequence by replacing the call to `return new Sequence()` with the code shown in Listing 2-1.

Listing 2-1. *Definition of the Sequence Activity*

```
return new Sequence()
{
    DisplayName = "Main Sequence",
    Variables = { numberBells, counter },
    Activities =
    {
        new WriteLine()
        {
            DisplayName = "Hello",
            Text = "Hello, World!"
        },
        new If()
        {
            DisplayName = "Adjust for PM"
            // Code to be added here in Level 2
        },
        new While()
        {
            DisplayName = "Sound Bells"
            // Code to be added here in Level 2
        },
        new WriteLine()
        {
            DisplayName = "Display Time",
```

```
            Text = "The time is: " + DateTime.Now.ToString()
        },
        new If()
        {
            DisplayName = "Greeting"
            // Code to be added here in Level 2
        }
    }
};
```

■ **Note** This implementation relies heavily on creating anonymous class instances. Classes such as Sequence, WriteLine, and If are instantiated but never named. This approach is similar to the technique called *functional construction*, which is used to build XML trees. If it seems strange to you, you might want to review some of the documentation on functional construction on MSDN.

This code first defines the DisplayName and associates the Variable objects with this activity. It then initializes the Activities member as a collection of activities. Specifically, it creates the activities shown in Table 2-1.

Table 2-1. *Activities*

Type	DisplayName
WriteLine	"Hello"
If	"Adjust for PM"
While	"Sound Bells"
WriteLine	"Display Time"
If	"Greeting"

For the WriteLine activities, the Text property is defined. For the remaining activities, the implementation of these will be defined in the next level.

Implementing Level 2

For the first If activity, enter the following code:

```
DisplayName = "Adjust for PM",
```

```
// Code to be added here in Level 2
Condition = ExpressionServices.Convert<bool>
    (env => numberBells.Get(env) > 12),
Then = new Assign<int>()
{
    DisplayName = "Adjust Bells"
    // Code to be added here in Level 3
}
```

This code defines the Condition and the Then properties (there is no Else branch). The Assign activity will be implemented in the next level. The definition of the Condition property, however, probably needs some explanation.

Expressions

The static Convert<T>() method of the ExpressionServices class is used to create an InArgument<T> class, which is what the Condition property is expecting. These classes and methods use the generic type (<T>) so they can be used for any data type. In this case, we need to use type bool because the Condition property of an If activity is expecting only true or false.

The expression is implemented by a lambda expression (similar to that used by LINQ syntax) to extract the data from the workflow environment. In a lambda expression, the => is referred to as the lambda operator. Parameters to the left are input parameters, and the actual expression is defined on the right side of the lambda operator. The value of env is supplied by the runtime when it tries to evaluate the Condition.

The workflow is actually stateless; it doesn't store any data elements. The Variable classes are simply data definitions. To get the actual data from a Variable class, you'll use its Get() method. This requires a token of sorts, which is an ActivityContext class. This is used to differentiate the values for this particular workflow instance from others that might be running concurrently. The value returned from Get(env) is then compared to see whether it's greater than 12.

Enter the following code for the While activity:

```
DisplayName = "Sound Bells",
// Code to be added here in Level 2
Condition = ExpressionServices.Convert<bool>
    (env => counter.Get(env) <= numberBells.Get(env)),
Body = new Sequence()
{
    DisplayName = "Sound Bell"
    // Code to be added here in Level 3
}
```

The Condition property on the While activity is identical to the If activity. It also uses the ExpressionServices class to create an InArgument<T> class, also of type bool. In this case, it is evaluating whether count <= numberBells. For both of these variables, it uses the Get(env) method to obtain the actual value.

For the second If activity (named "Greeting"), enter the following code:

```
DisplayName = "Greeting",
// Code to be added here in Level 2
Condition = ExpressionServices.Convert<bool>
    (env => DateTime.Now.Hour >= 18),
Then = new WriteLine() { Text = "Good Evening" },
Else = new WriteLine() { Text = "Good Day" }
```

For this Condition, the env input parameter is not used, but it must still be declared in the expression. The logic uses the current time to see whether it is past 6:00 PM. For both the Then and Else properties, a WriteLine activity is created. One says "Good Evening"; the other says "Good Day".

Implementing Level 3

For the first If activity (named "Adjust for PM"), you created a blank Assign activity in the Then property. Enter the following for its implementation:

```
DisplayName = "Adjust Bells",
// Code to be added here in Level 3
To = new OutArgument<int>(numberBells),
Value = new InArgument<int>(env => numberBells.Get(env) - 12)
```

Assign Activity

The Assign class is a generic, so it can support any data type. In this case, it is assigning integer values, so it was created as Assign<int>. The To and Value properties also use template classes and should be created with the same type (<int>). The To property is an OutArgument class, which takes a Variable class in its constructor. The Value property uses an InArgument class. You used this before for the If and While Condition property. For its constructor, it uses a lambda expression just as you did for the Condition property.

Sequence

In the While activity, you created an empty Sequence for the Execute property. This defines the sequence of activities that will be executed every time the while loop is iterated. Enter the following to populate the Activities property:

```
DisplayName = "Sound Bell",
// Code to be added here in Level 3
Activities =
{
    new WriteLine()
    {
        Text = new InArgument<string>(env => counter.Get(env).ToString())
    },
```

```
new Assign<int>()
{
    DisplayName = "Increment Counter",
    To = new OutArgument<int>(counter),
    Value = new InArgument<int>(env => counter.Get(env) + 1)
},
new Delay()
{
    Duration = TimeSpan.FromSeconds(1)
}
}
```

This code adds three activities to this Sequence:

- A WriteLine activity to display the counter
- An Assign activity to increment the counter
- A Delay activity to force a short pause between iterations

For this WriteLine activity, the Text property is not a literal string as the other ones were. In this case, the value to be displayed is defined as an expression. The Text property is expecting a string, so it creates an InArgument<string> class. By now, you're probably getting used to these lambda expressions. The Get(env) method of the Variable class provides the current value as an integer. The ToString() method converts it to a string.

For the Delay activity, the Duration property is passed as a TimeSpan class, which is created by the FromSeconds() static method.

Running the Application

Press F5 to run the application. Depending on the time of day, your results should look something like this:

```
Hello, World!
1
2
3
4
5
6
7
The time is: 10/5/2009 7:02:41 PM
Good Evening
Press ENTER to exit
```

The complete implementation of Program.cs is included in Listing 2-2.

Listing 2-2. Complete Solution Implementation (Program.cs)

```csharp
using System;
using System.Activities;
using System.Activities.Statements;
using System.Activities.Expressions;

namespace Chapter02
{
    class Program
    {
        static void Main(string[] args)
        {
            WorkflowInvoker.Invoke(CreateWorkflow());

            Console.WriteLine("Press ENTER to exit");
            Console.ReadLine();
        }

        static Activity CreateWorkflow()
        {
            Variable<int> numberBells = new Variable<int>()
            {
                Name = "numberBells",
                Default = DateTime.Now.Hour
            };
            Variable<int> counter = new Variable<int>()
            {
                Name = "counter",
                Default = 1
            };

            return new Sequence()
            {
                DisplayName = "Main Sequence",
                Variables = { numberBells, counter },
                Activities =
                {
                    new WriteLine()
                    {
                        DisplayName = "Hello",
```

```
        Text = "Hello, World!"
    },
    new If()
    {
        DisplayName = "Adjust for PM",
        // Code to be added here in Level 2
        Condition = ExpressionServices.Convert<bool>
            (env => numberBells.Get(env) > 12),
        Then = new Assign<int>()
        {
            DisplayName = "Adjust Bells",
            // Code to be added here in Level 3
            To = new OutArgument<int>(numberBells),
            Value = new InArgument<int>
                (env => numberBells.Get(env) - 12)
        }
    },
    new While()
    {
        DisplayName = "Sound Bells",
        // Code to be added here in Level 2
        Condition = ExpressionServices.Convert<bool>
            (env => counter.Get(env) <= numberBells.Get(env)),
        Body = new Sequence()
        {
            DisplayName = "Sound Bell",
            // Code to be added here in Level 3
            Activities =
            {
                new WriteLine()
                {
                    Text = new InArgument<string>
                        (env => counter.Get(env).ToString())
                },
                new Assign<int>()
                {
                    DisplayName = "Increment Counter",
                    To = new OutArgument<int>(counter),
                    Value = new InArgument<int>
                        (env => counter.Get(env) + 1)
                },
                new Delay()
                {
```

```
                              Duration = TimeSpan.FromSeconds(1)
                        }
                    }
                }
            },
            new WriteLine()
            {
                DisplayName = "Display Time",
                Text = "The time is: " + DateTime.Now.ToString()
            },
            new If()
            {
                DisplayName = "Greeting",
                // Code to be added here in Level 2
                Condition = ExpressionServices.Convert<bool>
                    (env => DateTime.Now.Hour >= 16),
                Then = new WriteLine() { Text = "Good Evening" },
                Else = new WriteLine() { Text = "Good Day" }
            }
        }
    };
    }
  }
}
```

Review

Some of the sample projects throughout this book will use the designer, whereas others will use a coded workflow. Using the designer will probably be initially easier than coded workflows. However, as you become more familiar with workflows, you might find that coded workflows are faster to write. The end result is the same, and either approach works fine.

CHAPTER 3

■ ■ ■

Flowchart Workflow

In this chapter, you'll create a workflow that uses the Flowchart activity. As its name suggests, a Flowchart activity works just like a flowchart; activities are connected together by decision trees. Using a Sequence activity, the child activities are executed in top-down (sequential) order. However, in a Flowchart activity, the child activities can be executed in any order, based on the decision branches.

Creating a Flowchart Workflow

Start by creating a new project/solution. Choose the Workflow Console Application template, as shown in Figure 3-1.

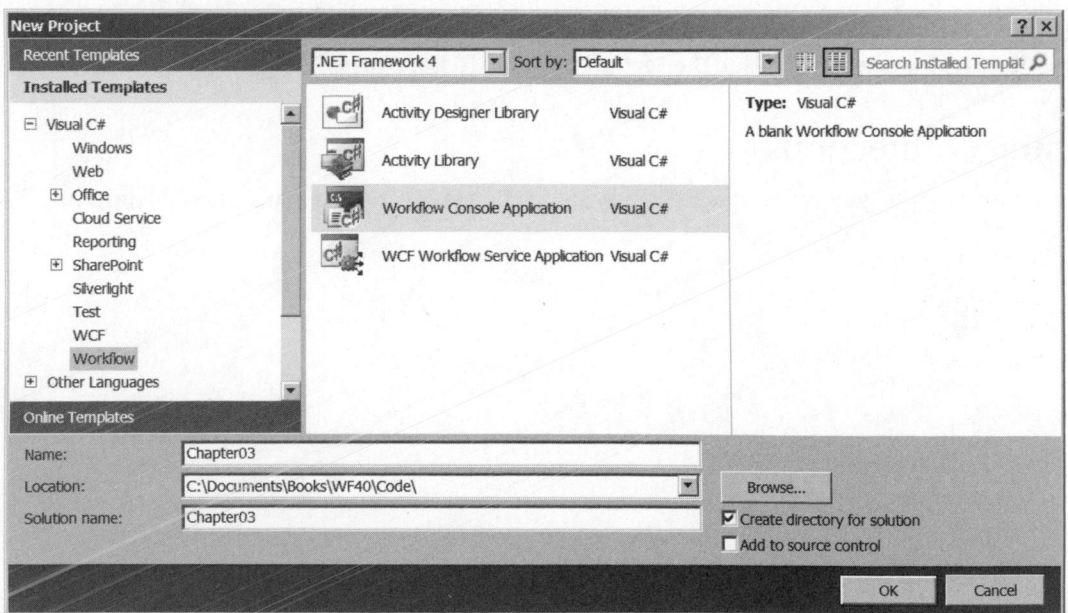

Figure 3-1. *Creating a flowchart workflow project*

Designing the Flowchart

Drag a Flowchart activity to the designer. The initial workflow diagram will be similar to the one shown in Figure 3-2. The green circle represents the starting node of your flowchart, and the empty space beneath it is where you will add the activities that make up your workflow.

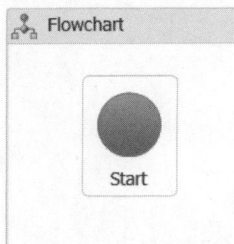

Figure 3-2. *Initial flowchart diagram*

The primary difference between a Flowchart activity and a Sequence activity is in how the child activities are connected. Recall from Chapter 1 that when you added activities to a Sequence, they were always executed in top-down order. You could control the order by rearranging the activities, but they were always aligned vertically and spaced evenly, and the arrows between the activities were drawn for you automatically. With a Flowchart activity, you can place the activities anywhere on the palette. And more importantly, you have to draw the arrows. But herein lies the power of the Flowchart activity; you can draw a connection back to a previous activity.

In this application, you will display an appropriate greeting based on the time of day. Start by displaying a standard greeting of "Hello, World!" To do this, drag a WriteLine activity below the green circle. Set the DisplayName to **Hello** and the Text property to **"Hello, World!"**.

Defining Connections

Roll the mouse over the green circle, and four gray connection points should appear (see Figure 3-3).

Figure 3-3. *Finding the beginning connection points*

Click one of these connection points and, holding the mouse button down, drag the mouse over the "Hello" activity until you see its connection points appear, as shown in Figure 3-4.

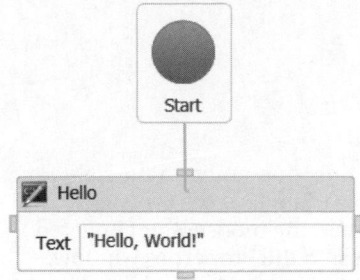

Figure 3-4. *Finding the ending connection points*

You don't have to select a connection point. As soon as you see the points appear, you'll know that the object has been selected. Let the mouse button up, and the two activities will be connected (see Figure 3-5).

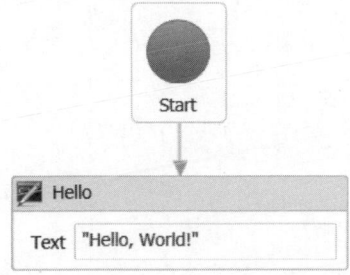

Figure 3-5. *Completed connection*

That's how you establish the connections between two activities. Hover over the predecessor until you see the connection points, click one, drag the mouse to the successor until you see its connection points, and let the mouse button up.

FlowDecision

Drag a FlowDecision activity below the "Hello" activity. The FlowDecision activity looks like a yellow diamond, much like a decision symbol in a normal flowchart diagram. In the Properties window, enter the *condition* as DateTime.Now.Hour >= 12. If you hover the mouse over the FlowDecision activity, you should see the connection points, as shown in Figure 3-6.

Figure 3-6. *FlowDecision activity*

There is a connection point on the left for the True branch and a connection point on the right for the False branch. The `Condition` is also displayed. Notice the small yellow triangle at the top-right corner. If you click it, the `Condition` property remains displayed, even when the mouse is not hovered over the activity. You can change the text for the True and False branches. In the Properties window, enter **Morning** for the `FalseLabel` property and **Afternoon** for the `TrueLabel` property. You should now see Morning and Afternoon when you hover the mouse over this activity.

First, connect the "Hello" activity to the `FlowDecision` activity by selecting a connection point on the "Hello" activity and dragging it to the `FlowDecision`. Then drag a `WriteLine` activity to the right of the `FlowDecision`. Set the `DisplayName` to **Morning** and the `Text` to **"Good Morning"**. Then hover over the `FlowDecision` and click the Morning connection point. Drag the mouse over the "Morning" activity until you see its connection points and let the mouse up. Your diagram should look like the one shown in Figure 3-7.

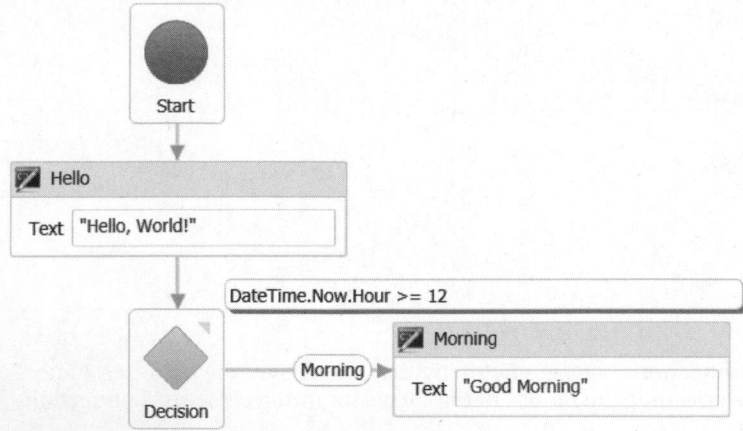

Figure 3-7. *Connecting the Morning branch*

■ **Note** The `DisplayName` property is not available on a `FlowDecision` activity. However, with the ability to display the `Condition` and to edit the True and False branches, the purpose of the activity should be evident in the diagram.

Drag another FlowDecision to the left of the first one. Set the Condition as **DateTime.Now.Hour >= 18**. Connect the Afternoon branch of the first FlowDecision to the new activity. Set the FalseLabel to **Afternoon** and the TrueLabel to **Evening**. Drag two WriteLine activities onto the workflow and name them **Afternoon** and **Evening**, and set the Text as **"Good Afternoon"** and **"Good Evening"**, respectively. Connect the Evening branch of the second FlowDecision to "Evening" and the Afternoon branch to "Afternoon". Your flowchart should look like the one shown in Figure 3-8.

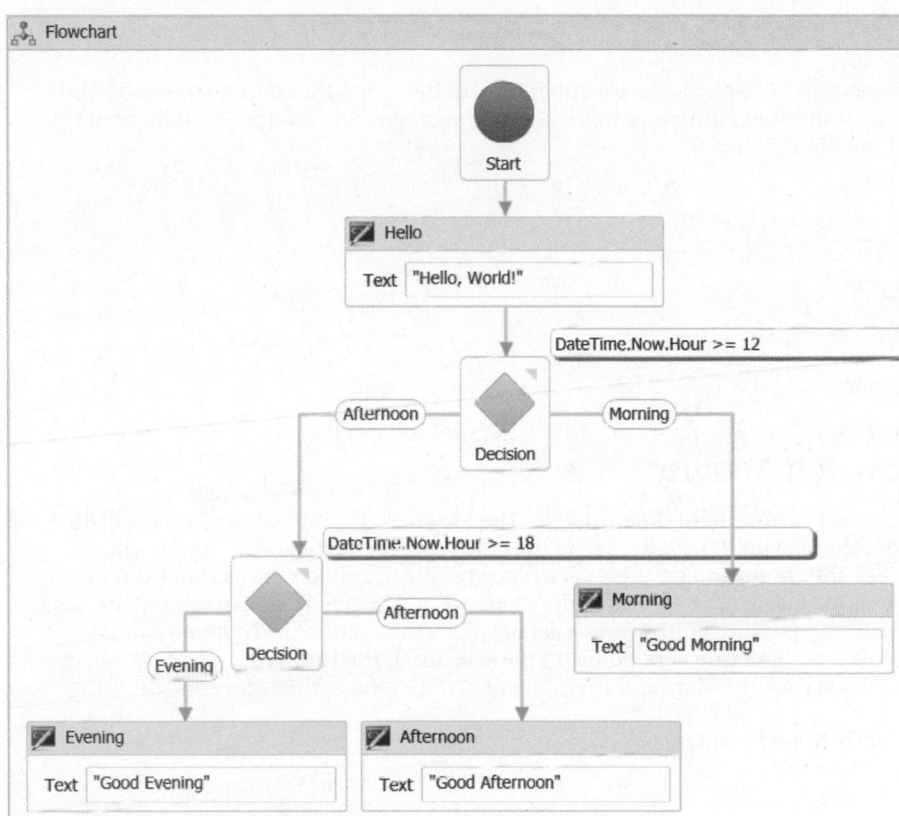

Figure 3-8. *Completed flowchart*

Running the Application

Before running the application, open the Program.cs file. This code is identical to the file generated in Chapter 1. Add the following code after the call to WorkflowInvoker class:

```
Console.WriteLine("Press ENTER to exit");
Console.ReadLine();
```

This keeps the console app from exiting before you can read the results. Press F5. Depending on the time of day, your results should be similar to the following:

```
Hello, World!
Good Evening
Press ENTER to exit
```

Flow Switch

A `FlowSwitch` activity works like a `FlowDecision` except instead of being restricted to a True and False branch, you can define an unlimited number of branches. It is analogous to a `switch` statement in C#. A `FlowSwitch` activity is shown in Figure 3-9.

Figure 3-9. *A FlowSwitch activity*

Adding a FlowSwitch Activity

Drag a `FlowSwitch` activity to the bottom of the workflow. The `FlowSwitch` activity is a template class (notice the `<T>` in the toolbox) so you'll need to specify the data type. It will default to `Int32`, which it what you'll need. Just click the OK button on the Select Types prompt. Draw a connection from the "Morning", "Afternoon", and "Evening" activities to the `FlowSwitch` activity. A `FlowSwitch` activity has a single property called `Expression`, which resolves to a set of values that define the branches. In this project, you'll display a different greeting depending on the season. In the Properties window, select the `Expression` property and then click the ellipses. Enter the following in the Expression editor:

```
CInt(((DateTime.Now.Month Mod 12) + 1) / 4)
```

■ **Note** The syntax of this expression might be surprising. All expressions in WF 4.0 use the Visual Basic syntax. Expressions are not compiled; they are evaluated by the workflow activities. So the syntax of the expressions is independent of the programming language used by the application. By convention, the VB syntax is used. To help you remember this, the `Expression` properties display the text "Enter a VB expression".

This expression approximates the season based on the current date. If the month is December, January, or February, the expression evaluates to 0. Similarly March, April, and May evaluate to 1. You will now create four branches; one for each season.

■ **Tip** When you hover the mouse over a `FlowSwitch` activity, the `Expression` will be displayed as shown in Figure 3-10. Just as with the `FlowDecision` activity, you can click on the yellow triangle and the `Expression` will remain displayed.

Figure 3-10. *Displaying the FlowSwitch expression*

Adding the FlowStep Activities

Each branch of a `FlowSwitch` activity is called a `FlowStep`. Although there is no `FlowStep` activity in the Toolbox, and you don't explicitly add these branches to the workflow, they are created internally as you draw connections from the `FlowSwitch` activity. Drag five `WriteLine` activities onto your workflow near the `FlowSwitch` activity. Set the `DisplayName` on each of these to **Winter**, **Spring**, **Summer**, **Autumn**, and **Default**. Draw a connection from the `FlowSwitch` to each of the `WriteLine` activities.

Click one of the connections. In the Properties window, you'll enter the `Case` value that determines when this case should be executed. For "Winter", the value should be **1**; for "Spring", it should be **2**, and so on. For the "Default" activity, leave the `Case` value blank and check the `IsDefaultCase` check box.

Your workflow should look like the one shown in Figure 3-11.

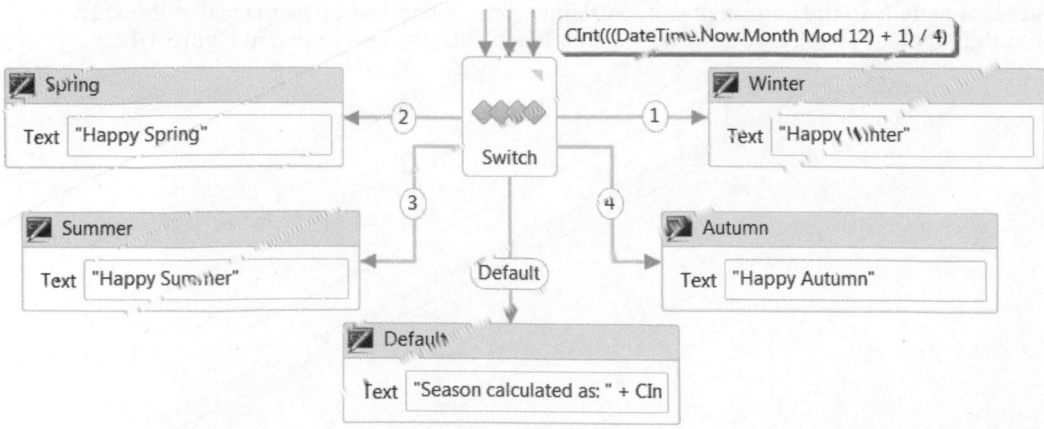

Figure 3-11. *FlowSwitch connections*

Enter an appropriate Text property on each of the WriteLine activities, such as **"Happy Summer"**. The "Default" activity should never be executed because you have defined a branch for each possible value of the Expression. However, it is useful to have it here in case there are problems with the Expression or any of the Case values. For the Text property on the "Default" activity, use the following:

```
"Season calculated as: " + CInt(((DateTime.Now.Month Mod 12) + 1) / 4).ToString()
```

Running the Application

Press F5 to run the application. Depending on the date and time, your results should be similar to these:

```
Hello, World!
Good Evening
Happy Summer!
Press ENTER to exit
```

Parallel

Before leaving this project, let me demonstrate the Parallel activity, which allows you to define a number of activity sequences that run in parallel. For this project, each of the branches will display a piece of information. The order that they are displayed is not important, so instead of executing them sequentially, you'll put them in a Parallel activity and execute them simultaneously.

Adding a Parallel Activity

Drag a Parallel activity to the bottom of your workflow. Draw a connection from each of the WriteLine activities to the Parallel activity. Your workflow should look like the one shown in Figure 3-12.

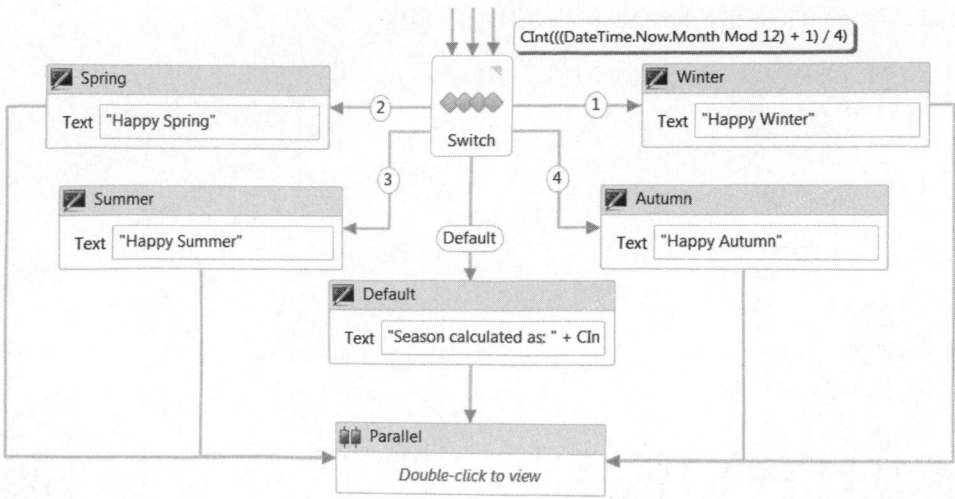

Figure 3-12. *Adding a Parallel activity*

Adding the Branches

Double-click the Parallel activity and drag three WriteLine activities onto it. One of these activities will display the date; another will display the time; and another will display the day of the week. Enter one of these expressions for the Text property on each of the WriteLine activities:

```
"Time: " + DateTime.Now.TimeOfDay.ToString()
"Date: " + DateTime.Now.Date.ToShortDateString()
"Today is: " + DateTime.Now.ToString("dddd")
```

The diagram should look like the one shown in Figure 3-13.

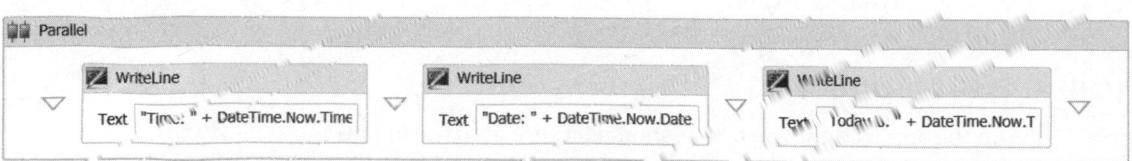

Figure 3-13. *Defining Parallel branches*

■ **Tip** The Parallel activity allows only a single activity in each branch. For this project, it works fine. However, if you need multiple activities in each branch, use a Sequence activity. Then you can add any number of activities onto it.

41

The final workflow should look like the one shown in Figure 3-14.

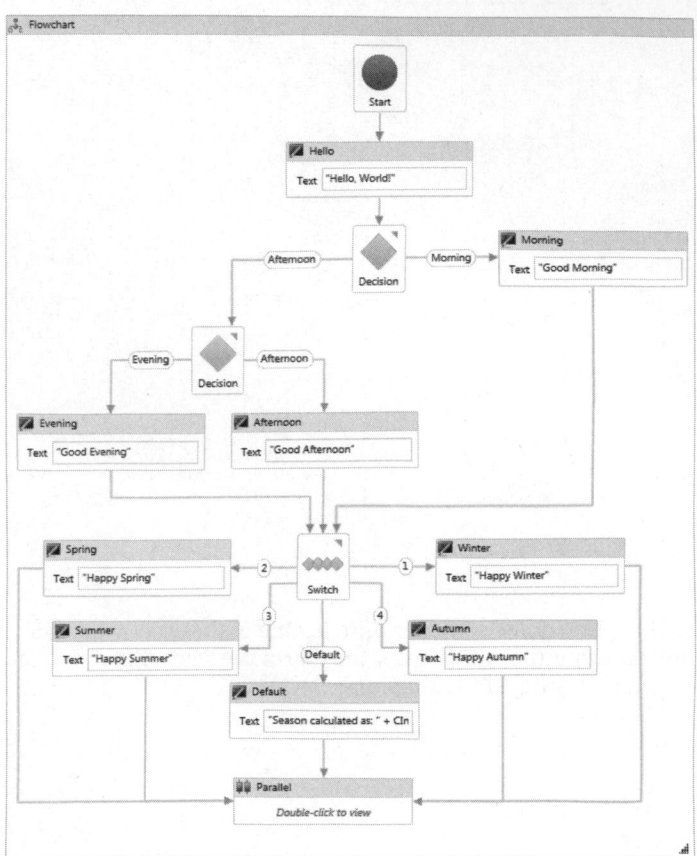

Figure 3-14. *Final flowchart workflow*

Running the Application

Press F5 to run the application. The results should be similar to the following:

```
Hello, World!
Good Evening
Happy Summer!
Time: 22:01:36.0594175
Date: 8/5/2009
Today is: Wednesday
Press ENTER to exit
```

Designing Workflows

So far, you have used the basic procedural and flowchart elements to design some simple workflows. In this section, you will learn some useful techniques that will help you build more complex workflows. You'll build a workflow that computes the total amount of an order. Each chapter will build upon the previous chapter and demonstrate new concepts along the way.

■ ■ ■

CHAPTER 4

Passing Arguments

In Chapter 1, I showed you how to define variables and arguments that will be used by the workflow. Using a coding analogy, variables are like class members, and arguments are similar to method parameters. You used variables in the last three chapters. In this chapter, you'll define both input and output arguments and pass them between the workflow and the host application.

Creating a New Solution

Start by creating a new Workflow Console Application, as shown in Figure 4-1. Name the project **OrderProcess**, and the solution **Chapter04**. You will be using the same project name in Chapters 5–7.

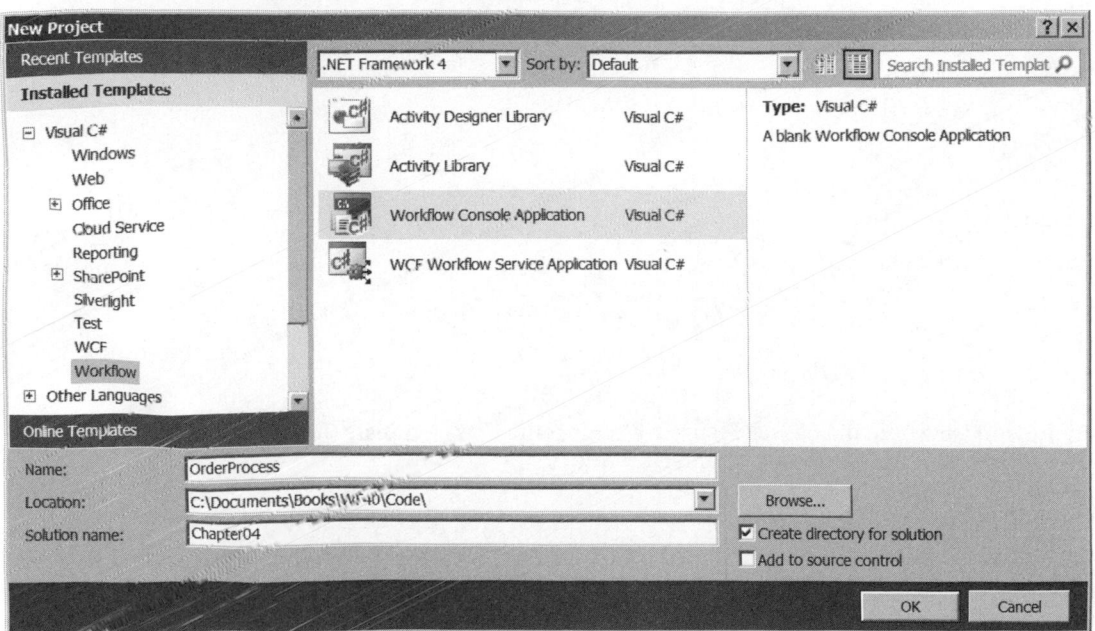

Figure 4-1. Creating a new sequential workflow project

In this project, you'll define an order for some products and pass that order into the workflow. The workflow will then compute the total cost of the order and return it to the application.

Defining the Order Class

The first step is to define the data structure that will contain the order details. In the Solution Explorer, right-click the project and choose Add ➤ Class, as shown in Figure 4-2.

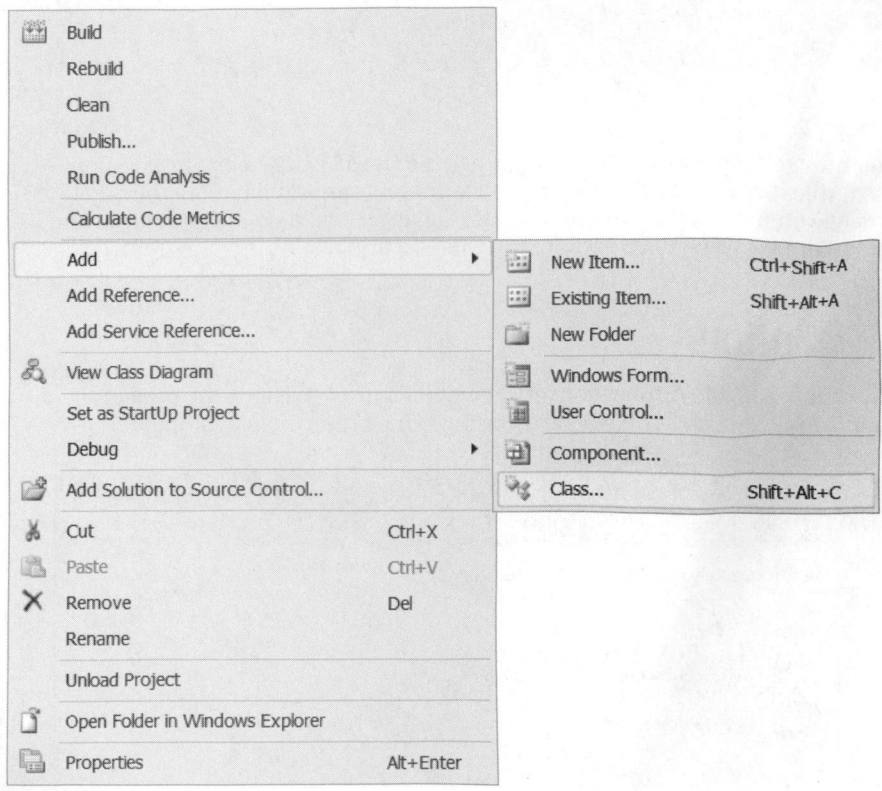

Figure 4-2. *Adding a class to the project*

In the Add New Item dialog (see Figure 4-3), select the Class template (it should be selected by default), specify the name as **Order.cs**, and click Add.

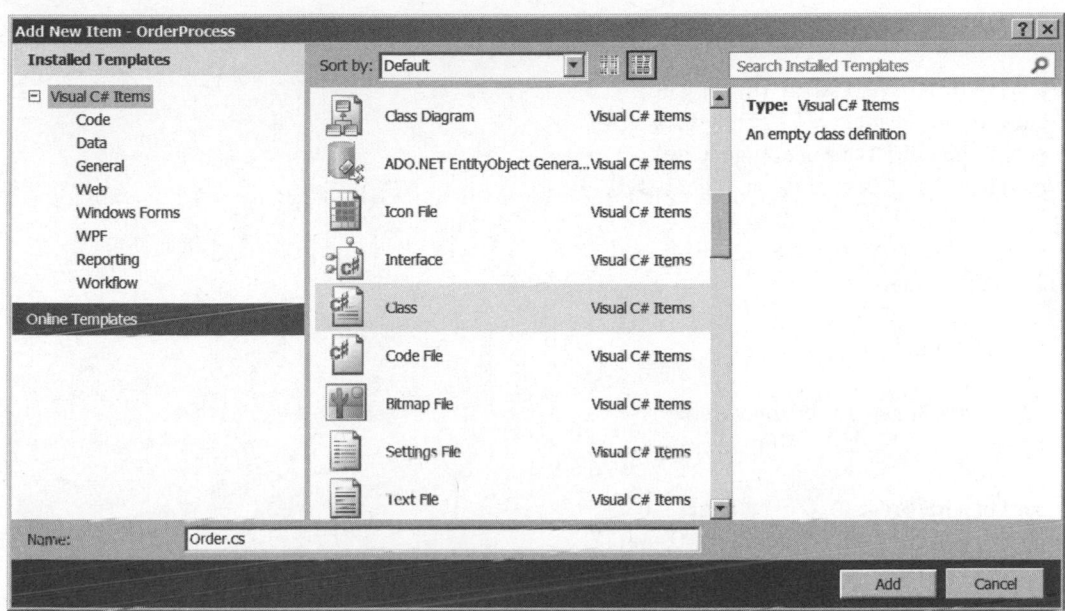

Figure 4-3. *Defining a new class*

The Solution Explorer should look like the one shown in Figure 4-4.

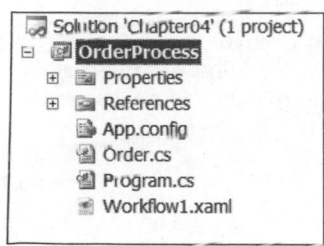

Figure 4-4. *Solution Explorer*

Enter the definition of the Order class, as shown in Listing 4-1.

Listing 4-1. *Order class*

```
using System;
using System.Collections.Generic;

namespace OrderProcess
```

```csharp
public class OrderItem
{
    public int OrderItemID { get; set; }
    public int Quantity { get; set; }
    public string ItemCode { get; set; }
    public string Description { get; set; }
}

public class Order
{
    public Order()
    {
        Items = new List<OrderItem>();
    }

    public int OrderID { get; set; }
    public string Description { get; set; }
    public decimal TotalWeight { get; set; }
    public string ShippingMethod { get; set; }

    public List<OrderItem> Items { get; set; }
}
}
```

The Order class contains a few public members (OrderID, Descripti ShippingMethod) plus a collection of OrderItem classes. These are the de determine the cost of the order. Build the solution by pressing F6. This will be available for the next step.

Implementing the Workflow

The solution template created a workflow file named Workflow1.xaml click the Workflow1.xaml file and choose Rename, as shown in Figur **OrderWF.xaml**.

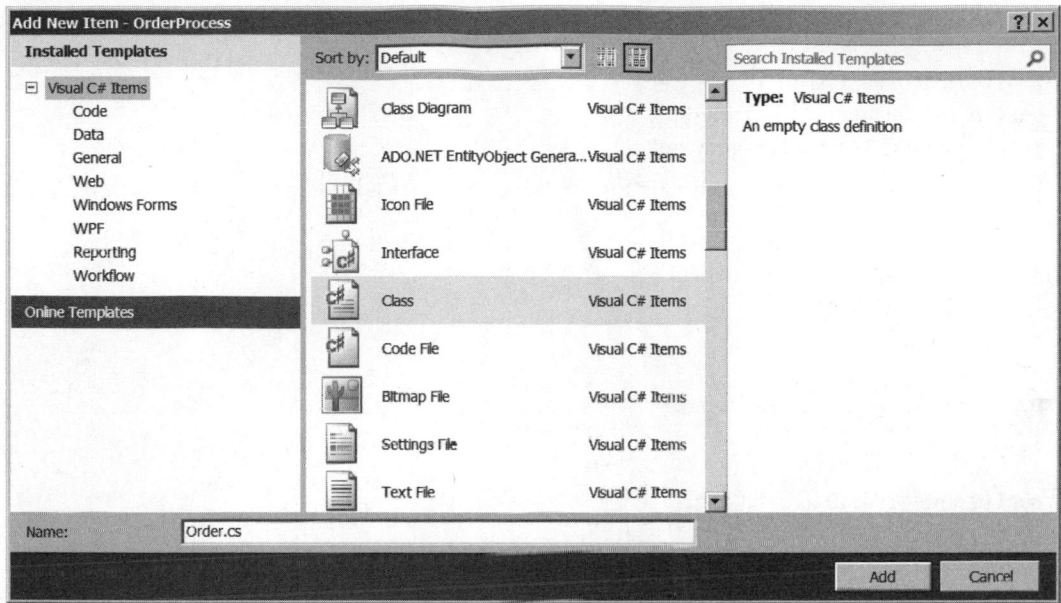

Figure 4-3. Defining a new class

The Solution Explorer should look like the one shown in Figure 4-4.

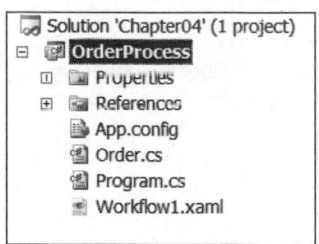

Figure 4-4. Solution Explorer

Enter the definition of the Order class, as shown in Listing 4-1.

Listing 4-1. *Order class*

```
using System;
using System.Collections.Generic;

namespace OrderProcess
{
```

```csharp
public class OrderItem
{
    public int OrderItemID { get; set; }
    public int Quantity { get; set; }
    public string ItemCode { get; set; }
    public string Description { get; set; }
}

public class Order
{
    public Order()
    {
        Items = new List<OrderItem>();
    }

    public int OrderID { get; set; }
    public string Description { get; set; }
    public decimal TotalWeight { get; set; }
    public string ShippingMethod { get; set; }

    public List<OrderItem> Items { get; set; }
}
}
```

The Order class contains a few public members (OrderID, Description, TotalWeight, and
ShippingMethod) plus a collection of OrderItem classes. These are the details the workflow wi
determine the cost of the order. Build the solution by pressing F6. This will compile the Ord
will be available for the next step.

Implementing the Workflow

The solution template created a workflow file named Workflow1.xaml. In the Solution Explo
click the Workflow1.xaml file and choose Rename, as shown in Figure 4-5. Change the nam
OrderWF.xaml.

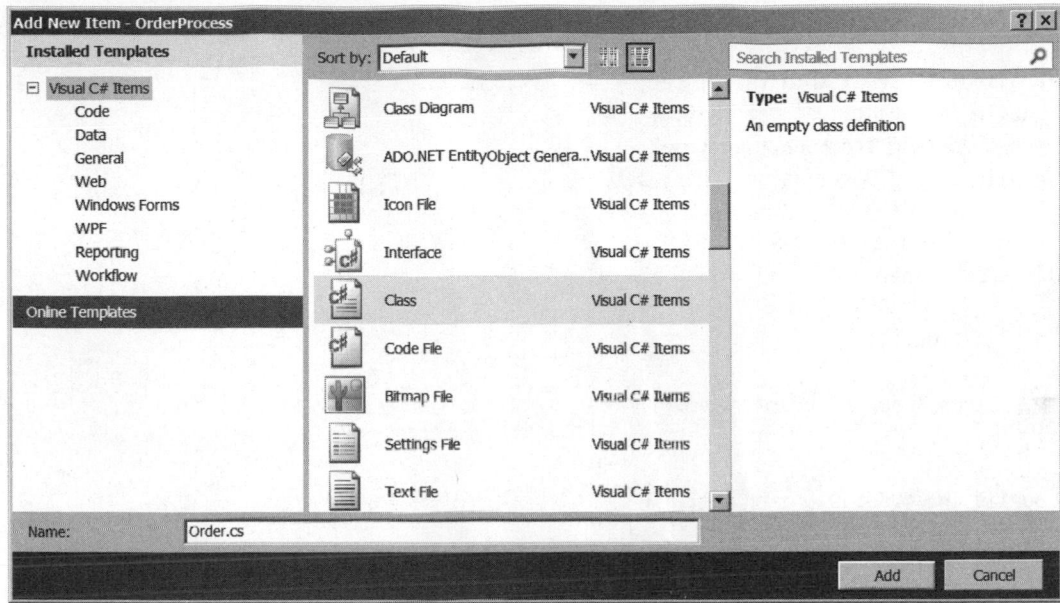

Figure 4-3. *Defining a new class*

The Solution Explorer should look like the one shown in Figure 4-4.

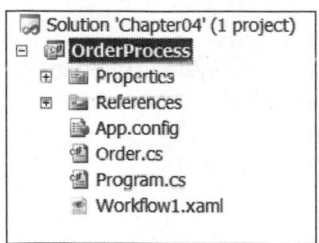

Figure 4-4. *Solution Explorer*

Enter the definition of the Order class, as shown in Listing 4-1.

Listing 4-1. *Order class*

```
using System;
using System.Collections.Generic;

namespace OrderProcess
{
```

```
public class OrderItem
{
    public int OrderItemID { get; set; }
    public int Quantity { get; set; }
    public string ItemCode { get; set; }
    public string Description { get; set; }
}

public class Order
{
    public Order()
    {
        Items = new List<OrderItem>();
    }

    public int OrderID { get; set; }
    public string Description { get; set; }
    public decimal TotalWeight { get; set; }
    public string ShippingMethod { get; set; }

    public List<OrderItem> Items { get; set; }
}
```

The Order class contains a few public members (OrderID, Description, TotalWeight, and ShippingMethod) plus a collection of OrderItem classes. These are the details the workflow will need to determine the cost of the order. Build the solution by pressing F6. This will compile the Order class s will be available for the next step.

Implementing the Workflow

The solution template created a workflow file named Workflow1.xaml. In the Solution Explorer, right click the Workflow1.xaml file and choose Rename, as shown in Figure 4-5. Change the name to **OrderWF.xaml**.

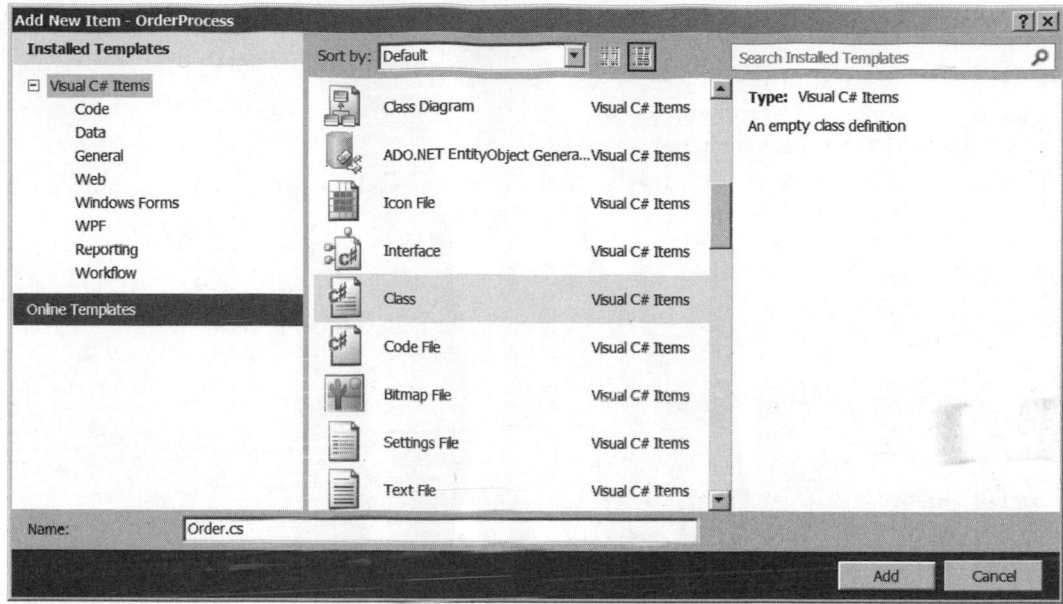

Figure 4-3. *Defining a new class*

The Solution Explorer should look like the one shown in Figure 4-4.

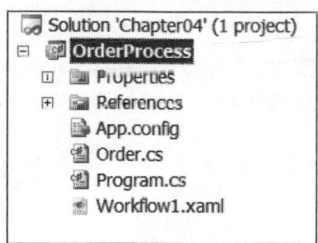

Figure 4-4. *Solution Explorer*

Enter the definition of the Order class, as shown in Listing 4-1.

Listing 4-1. *Order class*

```
using System;
using System.Collections.Generic;

namespace OrderProcess
{
```

```
public class OrderItem
{
    public int OrderItemID { get; set; }
    public int Quantity { get; set; }
    public string ItemCode { get; set; }
    public string Description { get; set; }
}

public class Order
{
    public Order()
    {
        Items = new List<OrderItem>();
    }

    public int OrderID { get; set; }
    public string Description { get; set; }
    public decimal TotalWeight { get; set; }
    public string ShippingMethod { get; set; }

    public List<OrderItem> Items { get; set; }
}
}
```

The Order class contains a few public members (OrderID, Description, TotalWeight, and ShippingMethod) plus a collection of OrderItem classes. These are the details the workflow will need to determine the cost of the order. Build the solution by pressing F6. This will compile the Order class so will be available for the next step.

Implementing the Workflow

The solution template created a workflow file named Workflow1.xaml. In the Solution Explorer, right click the Workflow1.xaml file and choose Rename, as shown in Figure 4-5. Change the name to **OrderWF.xaml**.

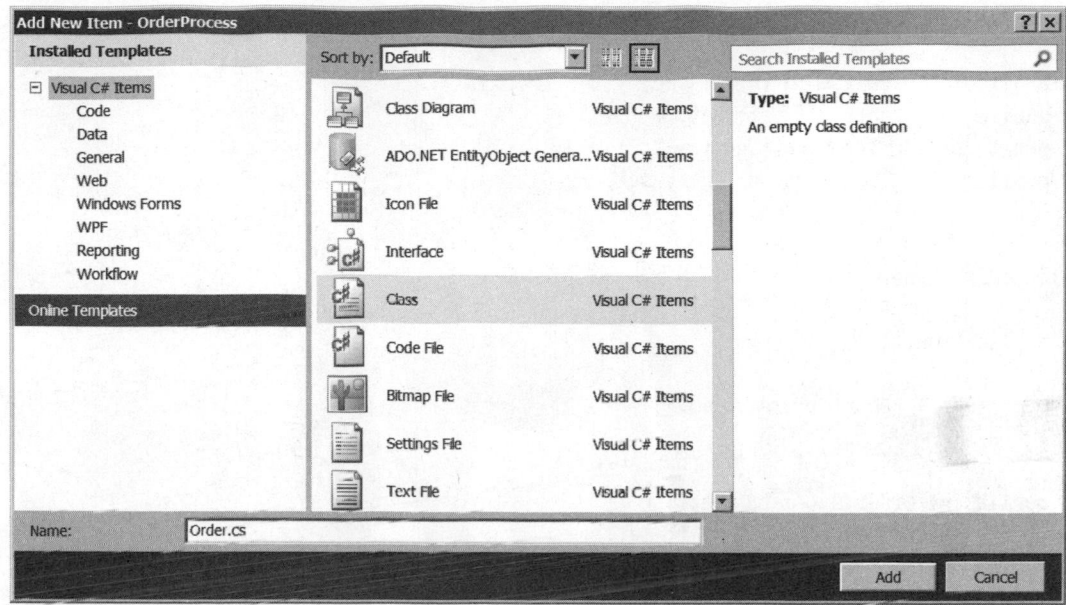

Figure 4-3. *Defining a new class*

The Solution Explorer should look like the one shown in Figure 4-4.

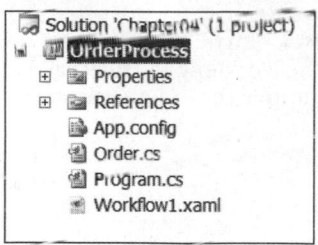

Figure 4-4. *Solution Explorer*

Enter the definition of the Order class, as shown in Listing 4-1.

Listing 4-1. *Order class*

```
using System;
using System.Collections.Generic;

namespace OrderProcess
{
```

```
public class OrderItem
{
    public int OrderItemID { get; set; }
    public int Quantity { get; set; }
    public string ItemCode { get; set; }
    public string Description { get; set; }
}

public class Order
{
    public Order()
    {
        Items = new List<OrderItem>();
    }

    public int OrderID { get; set; }
    public string Description { get; set; }
    public decimal TotalWeight { get; set; }
    public string ShippingMethod { get; set; }

    public List<OrderItem> Items { get; set; }
}
}
```

The Order class contains a few public members (OrderID, Description, TotalWeight, and ShippingMethod) plus a collection of OrderItem classes. These are the details the workflow will need determine the cost of the order. Build the solution by pressing F6. This will compile the Order class will be available for the next step.

Implementing the Workflow

The solution template created a workflow file named Workflow1.xaml. In the Solution Explorer, r click the Workflow1.xaml file and choose Rename, as shown in Figure 4-5. Change the name to **OrderWF.xaml**.

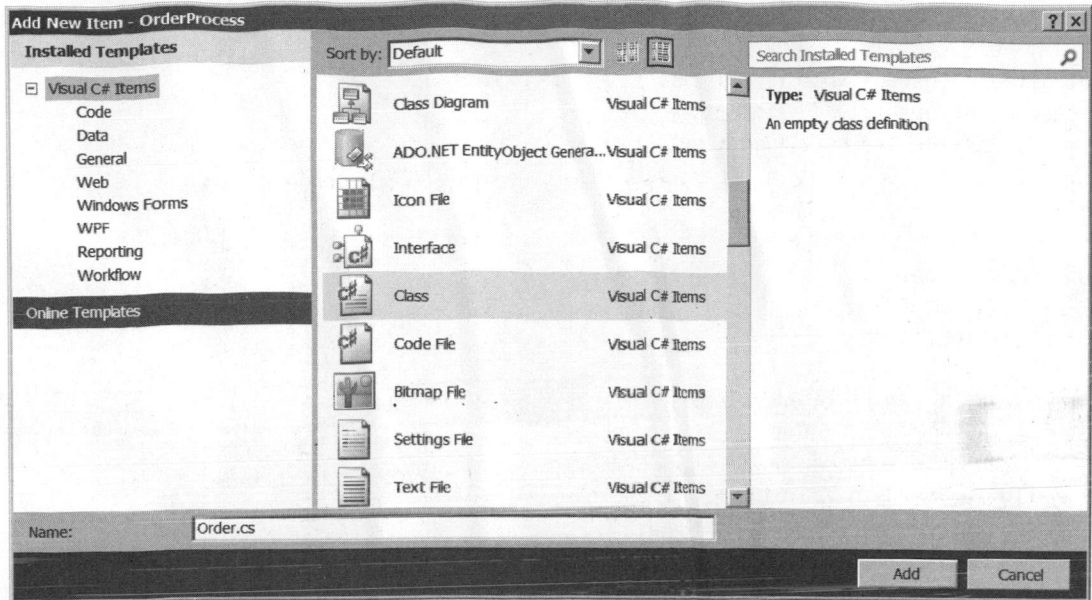

Figure 4-3. *Defining a new class*

The Solution Explorer should look like the one shown in Figure 4-4.

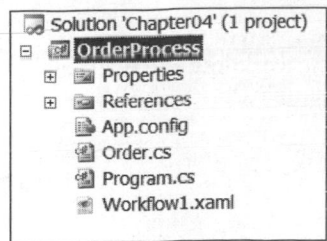

Figure 4-4. *Solution Explorer*

Enter the definition of the Order class, as shown in Listing 4-1.

Listing 4-1. *Order class*

```
using System;
using System.Collections.Generic;

namespace OrderProcess
{
```

```csharp
public class OrderItem
{
    public int OrderItemID { get; set; }
    public int Quantity { get; set; }
    public string ItemCode { get; set; }
    public string Description { get; set; }
}

public class Order
{
    public Order()
    {
        Items = new List<OrderItem>();
    }

    public int OrderID { get; set; }
    public string Description { get; set; }
    public decimal TotalWeight { get; set; }
    public string ShippingMethod { get; set; }

    public List<OrderItem> Items { get; set; }
}
}
```

The Order class contains a few public members (OrderID, Description, TotalWeight, and ShippingMethod) plus a collection of OrderItem classes. These are the details the workflow will need to determine the cost of the order. Build the solution by pressing F6. This will compile the Order class so it will be available for the next step.

Implementing the Workflow

The solution template created a workflow file named Workflow1.xaml. In the Solution Explorer, right-click the Workflow1.xaml file and choose Rename, as shown in Figure 4-5. Change the name to **OrderWF.xaml**.

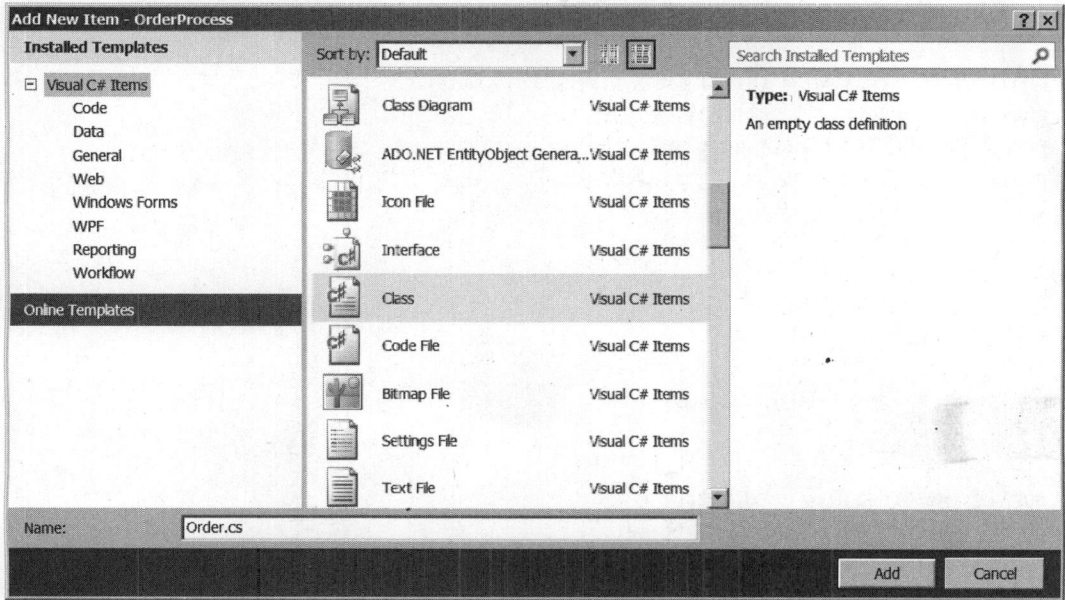

Figure 4-3. *Defining a new class*

The Solution Explorer should look like the one shown in Figure 4-4.

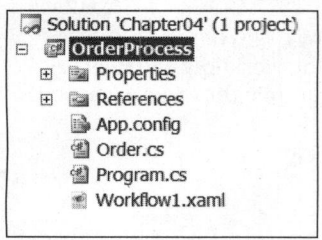

Figure 4-4. *Solution Explorer*

Enter the definition of the Order class, as shown in Listing 4-1.

Listing 4-1. *Order class*

```
using System;
using System.Collections.Generic;

namespace OrderProcess
{
```

```
public class OrderItem
{
    public int OrderItemID { get; set; }
    public int Quantity { get; set; }
    public string ItemCode { get; set; }
    public string Description { get; set; }
}

public class Order
{
    public Order()
    {
        Items = new List<OrderItem>();
    }

    public int OrderID { get; set; }
    public string Description { get; set; }
    public decimal TotalWeight { get; set; }
    public string ShippingMethod { get; set; }

    public List<OrderItem> Items { get; set; }
}
}
```

The Order class contains a few public members (OrderID, Description, TotalWeight, and ShippingMethod) plus a collection of OrderItem classes. These are the details the workflow will need to determine the cost of the order. Build the solution by pressing F6. This will compile the Order class so it will be available for the next step.

Implementing the Workflow

The solution template created a workflow file named Workflow1.xaml. In the Solution Explorer, right-click the Workflow1.xaml file and choose Rename, as shown in Figure 4-5. Change the name to **OrderWF.xaml**.

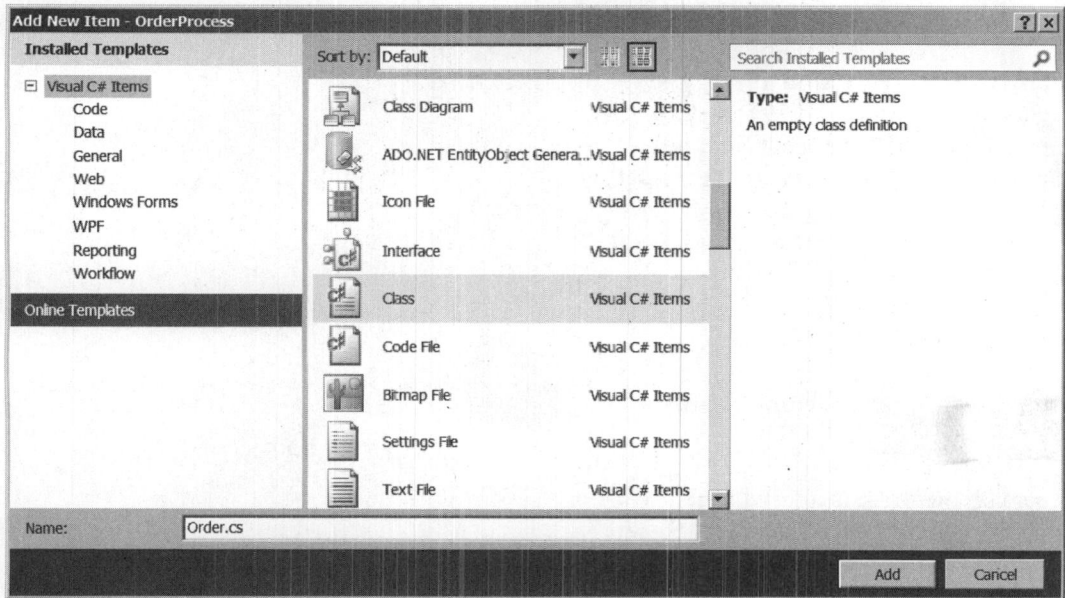

Figure 4-3. Defining a new class

The Solution Explorer should look like the one shown in Figure 4-4.

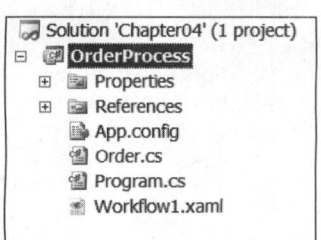

Figure 4-4. Solution Explorer

Enter the definition of the Order class, as shown in Listing 4-1.

Listing 4-1. *Order class*

```
using System;
using System.Collections.Generic;

namespace OrderProcess
{
```

47

```
public class OrderItem
{
    public int OrderItemID { get; set; }
    public int Quantity { get; set; }
    public string ItemCode { get; set; }
    public string Description { get; set; }
}

public class Order
{
    public Order()
    {
        Items = new List<OrderItem>();
    }

    public int OrderID { get; set; }
    public string Description { get; set; }
    public decimal TotalWeight { get; set; }
    public string ShippingMethod { get; set; }

    public List<OrderItem> Items { get; set; }
}
}
```

The Order class contains a few public members (OrderID, Description, TotalWeight, and ShippingMethod) plus a collection of OrderItem classes. These are the details the workflow will need to determine the cost of the order. Build the solution by pressing F6. This will compile the Order class so it will be available for the next step.

Implementing the Workflow

The solution template created a workflow file named Workflow1.xaml. In the Solution Explorer, right-click the Workflow1.xaml file and choose Rename, as shown in Figure 4-5. Change the name to **OrderWF.xaml**.

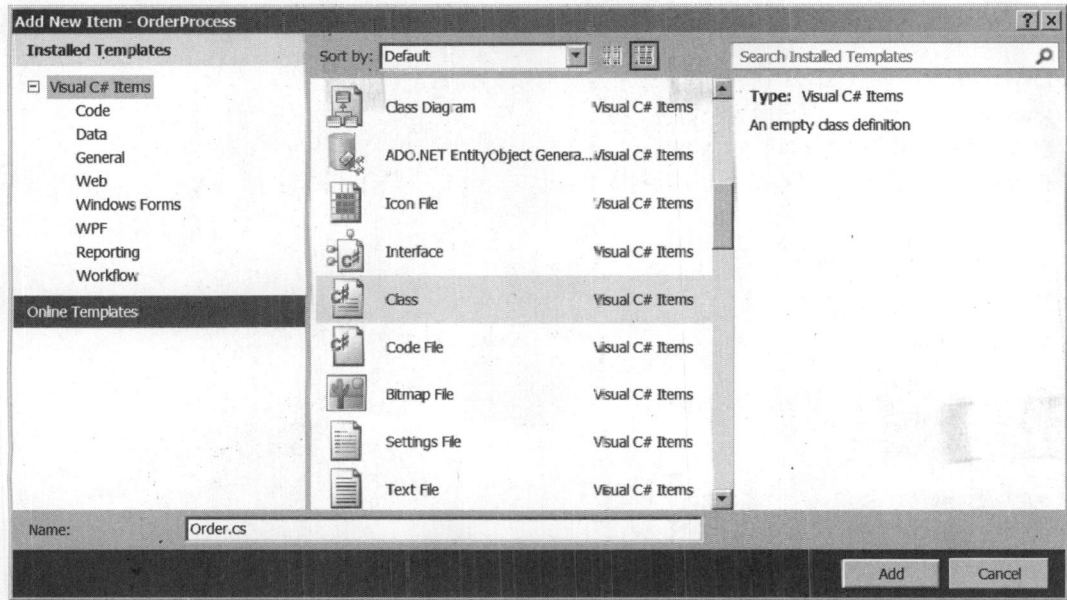

Figure 4-3. *Defining a new class*

The Solution Explorer should look like the one shown in Figure 4-4.

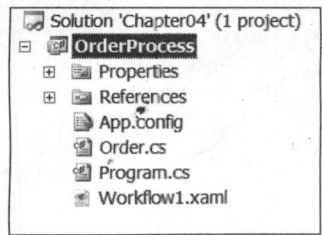

Figure 4-4. *Solution Explorer*

Enter the definition of the Order class, as shown in Listing 4-1.

Listing 4-1. *Order class*

```csharp
using System;
using System.Collections.Generic;

namespace OrderProcess
{
```

```
public class OrderItem
{
    public int OrderItemID { get; set; }
    public int Quantity { get; set; }
    public string ItemCode { get; set; }
    public string Description { get; set; }
}

public class Order
{
    public Order()
    {
        Items = new List<OrderItem>();
    }

    public int OrderID { get; set; }
    public string Description { get; set; }
    public decimal TotalWeight { get; set; }
    public string ShippingMethod { get; set; }

    public List<OrderItem> Items { get; set; }
}
}
```

The Order class contains a few public members (OrderID, Description, TotalWeight, and ShippingMethod) plus a collection of OrderItem classes. These are the details the workflow will need to determine the cost of the order. Build the solution by pressing F6. This will compile the Order class so it will be available for the next step.

Implementing the Workflow

The solution template created a workflow file named Workflow1.xaml. In the Solution Explorer, right-click the Workflow1.xaml file and choose Rename, as shown in Figure 4-5. Change the name to **OrderWF.xaml**.

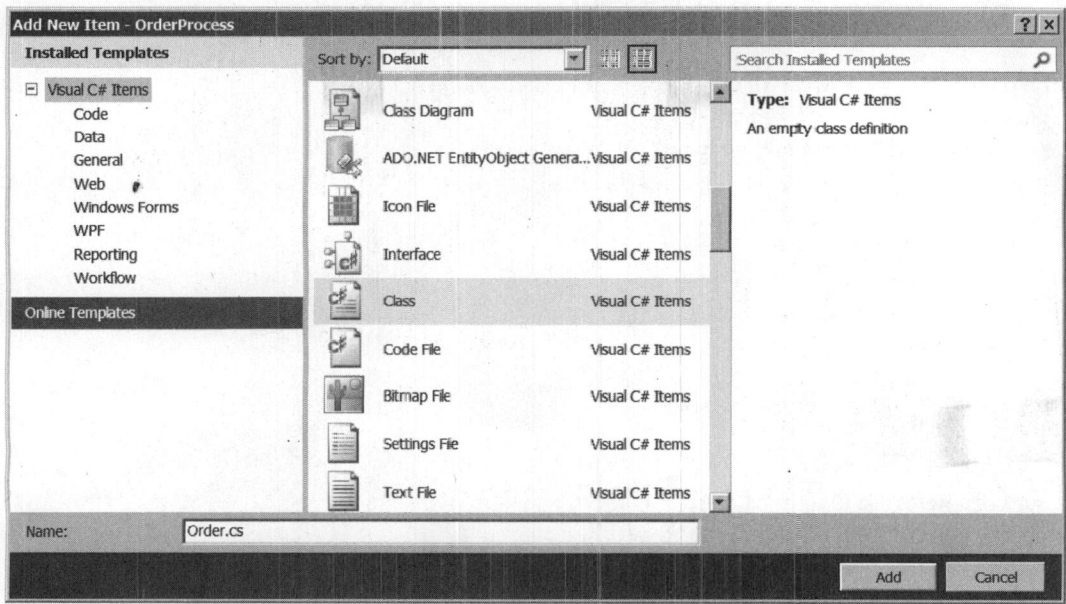

Figure 4-3. *Defining a new class*

The Solution Explorer should look like the one shown in Figure 4-4.

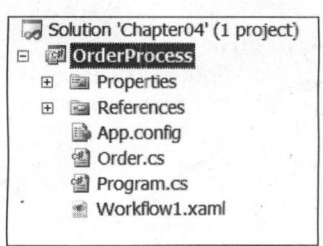

Figure 4-4. *Solution Explorer*

Enter the definition of the Order class, as shown in Listing 4-1.

Listing 4-1. *Order class*

```csharp
using System;
using System.Collections.Generic;

namespace OrderProcess
{
```

```csharp
public class OrderItem
{
    public int OrderItemID { get; set; }
    public int Quantity { get; set; }
    public string ItemCode { get; set; }
    public string Description { get; set; }
}

public class Order
{
    public Order()
    {
        Items = new List<OrderItem>();
    }

    public int OrderID { get; set; }
    public string Description { get; set; }
    public decimal TotalWeight { get; set; }
    public string ShippingMethod { get; set; }

    public List<OrderItem> Items { get; set; }
}
}
```

The Order class contains a few public members (OrderID, Description, TotalWeight, and ShippingMethod) plus a collection of OrderItem classes. These are the details the workflow will need to determine the cost of the order. Build the solution by pressing F6. This will compile the Order class so it will be available for the next step.

Implementing the Workflow

The solution template created a workflow file named Workflow1.xaml. In the Solution Explorer, right-click the Workflow1.xaml file and choose Rename, as shown in Figure 4-5. Change the name to **OrderWF.xaml**.

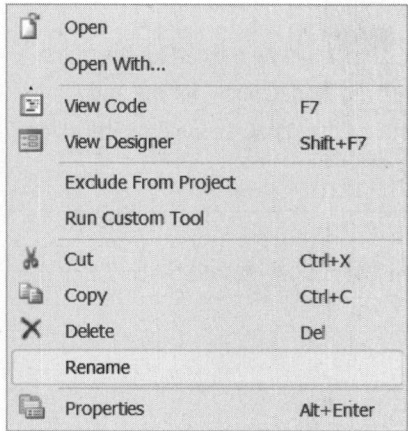

Figure 4-5. *Renaming the workflow file*

You will also need to open the OrderWF.xaml in code view. In the first line, change the Class attribute to this:

```
x:Class="OrderProcess.OrderWF"
```

Defining the Arguments

Open the OrderWF.xaml file (in design mode). You will now define the arguments into and out of the workflow. Click the Argument button at the bottom left of the workflow designer. An empty collection of arguments should be displayed, as shown in Figure 4-6.

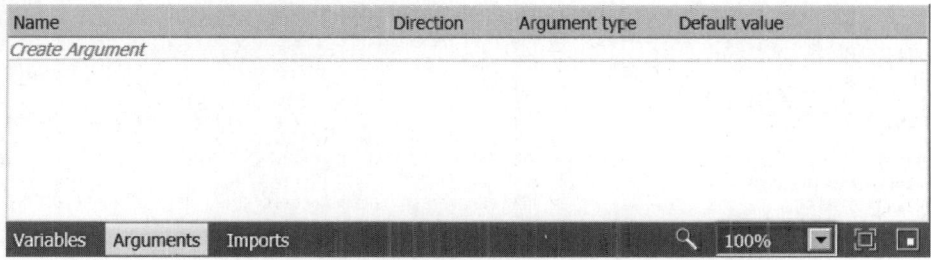

Figure 4-6. *The initial (empty) Arguments list*

■ **Tip** You might recall from Chapter 1 that variables had a specified scope. They could be defined for the entire workflow or for a specific activity (and its descendants). Arguments, however, are by definition, for the entire workflow because they define data passed to and from the workflow. Therefore, there is no Scope property when defining an argument.

Click the *Create Argument* link. Enter the Name as **OrderInfo**. The Direction should be In. Click the ArgumentType and expand the drop-down menu, shown in Figure 4-7.

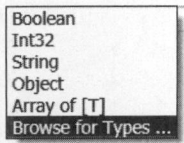

Figure 4-7. The ArgumentType drop-down menu

Select the last entry (Browse for Types). This will display the dialog shown in Figure 4-8.

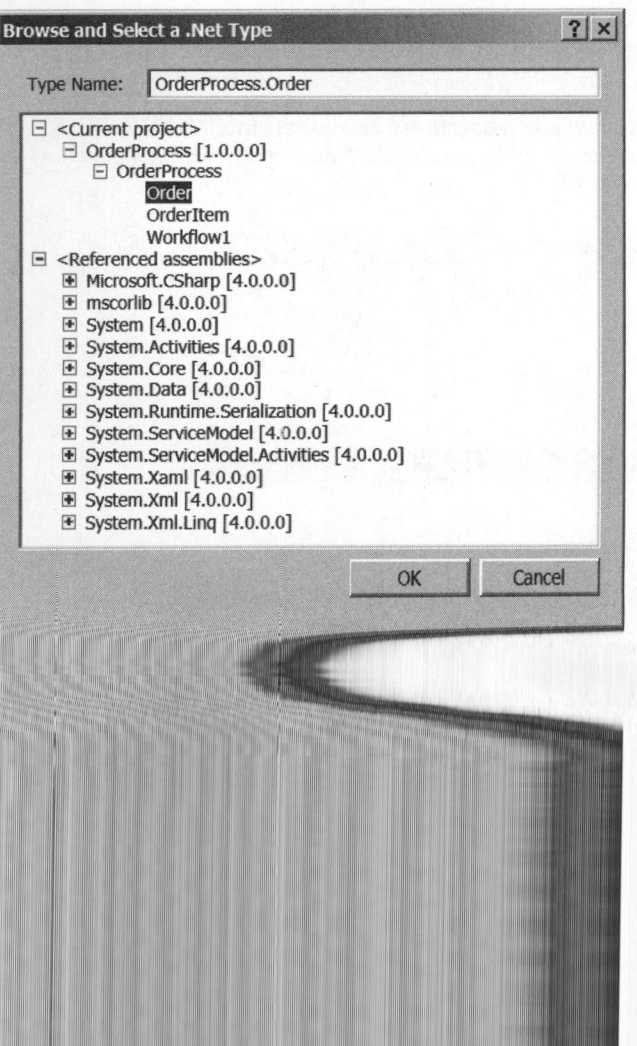